Louis Golding has spent almost the whole of his adult life in the field of local government—as a local government officer with the LCC (later the GLC) and for fourteen years as a London borough councillor. He is the author of *A Dictionary of Local Government in England and Wales*, published in 1962, and for several years was a London University extension lecturer in local government. He has acted as an examiner in local government to the GLC for their administrative staff and as an examiner in general knowledge to the Civil Service Commission. In recent years he has extended his interests to spheres that relate to central as well as local government and to the social services, serving as a member of Rent Tribunals and Rent Assessment Committees, Industrial Tribunals, Mental Health Review Tribunals, the Immigration Appeal Tribunal and the Middlesex Executive Council; he is currently Chairman of a Housing Association for elderly people. His wife has devoted a great deal of her time and energy to voluntary social work, including mental health welfare and the chairmanship of a workroom for the elderly. They have a son and daughter (both married) and a grand-daughter. His main recreation, apart from his family interests, is travelling—in this country and abroad.

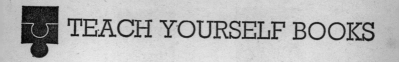
TEACH YOURSELF BOOKS

LOCAL GOVERNMENT

L. Golding, LL.B.

TEACH YOURSELF BOOKS

HODDER & STOUGHTON

ST PAUL'S HOUSE   WARWICK LANE   LONDON EC4P 4AH

First printed 1955
Second edition 1959
Third edition 1964
Fourth edition 1970
Fifth edition 1975

ISBN 0 340 19820 6

Printed and bound in Great Britain for Teach Yourself Books,
Hodder & Stoughton, by Cox & Wyman Ltd, London, Reading
and Fakenham

Contents

6 *Contents*

Preface

The object of this book is to present in a simple and concise form a conspectus of the local government system of England and Wales, and to stimulate a general interest in local representative institutions. I have endeavoured to sketch the development of local government, to explain its principal features and to deal with a few of its most controversial issues.

It is hoped that the book will appeal to four classes of readers: the student who is preparing for a local government examination; the local government employee who wishes to take a wider and more intelligent interest in his daily duties; the elected member of a local authority or the co-opted member of a committee; and the general reader, who may have little or no knowledge of the ramifications of local government, but has a desire to acquire an understanding of its main principles.

The first two editions of this book included chapters on Scotland and Northern Ireland and on Local Government Abroad. The chapter on Local Government Abroad was deleted from the third edition, and the fourth edition contained no reference to Scotland and Northern Ireland. The omission of Scotland and Northern Ireland from the last two editions is regretted, but I feel that it can be justified on the ground that within the compass of this small book the space which could be devoted to these two countries would be sufficient for only sketchy and inadequate treatment.

Since the publication of the fourth edition there has been a fundamental transformation of the structure of local government and important developments in almost every other sphere. My aim has been to incorporate in the present edition the substance of all these changes, and, as far as possible, to bring the book up to date.

L.G.

1 Historical Background

The nature of local government and its relation to central government

Local government has been defined in various ways, but perhaps the simplest definition is the management of their own affairs by the people of a locality. We sometimes speak of the local Inspector of Taxes and the local postmaster, and at first sight the use of the word local in this context may suggest a reference to local authorities; but care must be taken not to confuse local authorities with members of a national organisation operating within a locality. Local authorities, although subject to some degree of supervision and control by the central government, are autonomous bodies with freedom to decide questions of policy for themselves, and an essential feature of local government is that members of local authorities are elected by the inhabitants of the area. The Inspector of Taxes, however, is an officer, not of an elective local authority, but a civil servant employed by the Board of Inland Revenue, a central government department responsible for the assessment and collection of certain direct taxes. Similarly, the local postmaster is an officer of the Post Office, which in 1969 ceased to be a government department and became a public corporation. Neither the Inspector of Taxes nor the local postmaster has any direct connection with local government. It is clear, therefore, that an officer of the central government or of a public corporation, even if he is concerned with the administration of a service within a defined locality, is not a local authority or an officer of a local authority.

A study of the present system of local government is greatly facilitated by a knowledge of the development of local government from earlier times. Although most of the major local authorities in existence today are of recent origin, and their constitution, powers and duties were laid down by modern statutes, the structure of local government is still, to some extent, based on areas of administration which existed in Saxon or Norman times, and some of the functions for which local authorities are now responsible were exercised in a rudimentary form in the Middle Ages.

The medieval county organisation

When William the Conqueror ascended the throne of England in 1066 the country was divided into counties or shires, each of which was governed by a shire-reeve or sheriff, who was appointed by the King. In Norman times the authority of the sheriff was so extensive that he has been described as 'a provincial viceroy'. Usually a landowner of the county, he collected the income arising from the King's estates and other royal dues, including various judicial payments, and looked after the King's interests. But although the sheriff was a royal dignitary, and sometimes acted despotically, his power was circumscribed by the existence of a shire-moot or county court, consisting of all the freemen of the county, held two or three times a year and presided over by the sheriff. The functions of the county court were not solely judicial: the court not only dealt with criminal charges but was also used by the King for the extraction of local information—e.g. for establishing a title to land or for inquiring into the conduct of an official.

Each county was divided into hundreds,[1] and in each

---

[1] In some parts of the country the area corresponding to the hundred was known as the wapentake.

hundred there was a hundred court, which was held monthly. It consisted of the freeholders of the hundred, presided over by an official, known as a bailiff, who was appointed by the sheriff. The hundred court settled disputes relating to land, and was also responsible for the enforcement of a primitive criminal law system known as frankpledge. Under the frankpledge system all men were required to group themselves into tithings (groups of ten), and the men of each tithing were held mutually responsible for each other's good behaviour. It was part of the sheriff's duty to hold an inspection (known as the sheriff's tourn) at each hundred court twice a year, in order to ensure that each tithing was at full strength, that every man was in a tithing and that any member of a tithing who had committed an offence was duly punished.

The boroughs

The smallest area in the medieval local government hierarchy was the vill or township, and each vill or township was represented at the sheriff's tourn by its reeve and four best men. Frequently the area of the vill coincided with that of the manor, a feudal unit within which the lord of the manor, as the result of a royal grant, sometimes exercised criminal jurisdiction to the exclusion of the sheriff and the county organisation. Some of the more populous of these vills, particularly those where trade was carried on, succeeded in obtaining from the King, in return for a money payment, privileges of a far wider character. A valuable concession frequently made by the King was the right to administer justice, either civil or criminal. This was a concession of great value as the fees and fines levied were payable to the governing body of the town. Important privileges conferred on the inhabitants of a town by the King were embodied in a Royal Charter, and the possession of such a Charter was later a deciding factor in determining whether a town was to be regarded as a borough. The question of whether or not a town was a borough assumed added importance when each borough became a parliamentary constituency with the right to return members to the House of Commons.

The rise of the justice of the peace

In the later Middle Ages the sheriff declined in importance, and the county court fell into decay. By the time of the Tudors the sheriff had been superseded as the chief local government functionary of the county by the justices of the peace. These justices of the peace, who were first appointed in the reign of Edward III, were entrusted with both judicial and administrative duties of a very varied character. The Black Death (1348–9) left the country in a parlous economic state, and it was the justices of the peace who were assigned the difficult task of enforcing the labour legislation which was enacted following this great catastrophe. In the reign of Elizabeth I, when a system was evolved for the relief of the poor from public funds, the Government of the day turned to the justices of the peace to secure the effective administration of its new policy. As we shall see later, the office of justice of the peace assumed even greater importance in the eighteenth century, when the local justice became the pivot of county and parochial government.

The heyday of parish government

During the seventeenth century and the greater part of the eighteenth century English local government was to a large extent parochial government. The chief function of local government was the relief of destitution, and this was a parish responsibility. The country, which was still pre-dominantly agricultural in character, was divided into about 15 000 parishes, most of which contained scattered populations of farming communities. In the typical English parish, consisting perhaps of two or three score families, the inhabitants who formed the vestry (governing body) would meet at Easter. The vestry would probably consist of the squire, the clergyman, the innkeeper and a few farmers. The vestry was, therefore, not in any sense a body representative of all the inhabitants.

The officers of the parish were the churchwardens, constable, surveyors of highways and overseers of the poor. As these officers were unpaid and service was compulsory, it is not surprising that, except in the case of the office of churchwarden, which was one of some dignity, there was a strong reluctance on the part of the parishioners to accept the burden of office. The parish, which often coincided in area with the vill or township, was a centre of population surrounding a church, and the functions of the two, three or four churchwardens were both ecclesiastical and civil. They were elected annually by the vestry, and were concerned not only with such duties as the repair and decoration of the church and the allocation of seats in the church but also, in conjunction with the overseers, with the relief of the poor. The parish constable, who was first mentioned in the Statute of Winchester (1285), was appointed by the justices and was required, in accordance with their directions, to maintain law and order within the parish. The two surveyors of highways were selected by the justices from a list of persons submitted by the parish vestry. With certain exceptions, each parishioner was required to do six days a year statute labour on the roads, and it was the duty of these surveyors of highways to ensure that this statute labour was carried out and to levy a fine in default. The two, three or four parishioners who were selected as overseers of the poor by the justices were concerned with the relief of the destitute, the removal of paupers to other parishes and the binding of apprentices. The constable, surveyors of highways and overseers of the poor worked under the close supervision of the local justices.

The golden age of the justices of the peace

When one examines the multifarious duties of the local justices of the peace during the eighteenth century one is not surprised that they have been referred to as 'judicial beasts of burden' and 'maids of all work'. Justices of the peace were appointed by the Lord Chancellor on the nomination of the Lord Lieutenant[1] of the County. Their duties were administrative, judicial and even legislative. These unpaid amateurs, who met at Quarter Sessions four times a year, were responsible for the repair of bridges, the enforcement of highway repairs against defaulting parishes and the management of the county gaol. They heard appeals from Petty Sessions (two or more justices sitting for a division of the county) against rate assessments, the apprenticeship of paupers and appointments to parochial offices. Their duties also included the fixing of wages and prices, and, at the end of the eighteenth century, the fixing of standard scales of poor relief. Moreover, the local justice of the peace exercised minor jurisdiction as an individual in his own parlour and, with one or more brother justices sitting in Petty Sessions, could deal with a very wide range of judicial and administrative work, including minor criminal offences and appeals from paupers against the refusal of overseers to grant relief. In Special Sessions—i.e. meetings of justices for special functions—the justices for a division of the county would deal with such matters as the granting of licences to alehouses.

In rural areas the typical justice was the local squire or clergyman. A few of the justices were enlightened administrators, but many of them were narrow-minded and inefficient, and as Catholics, strict Nonconformists and persons engaged in trade were excluded from the Bench, justices had perforce to be appointed from the landed gentry and clergy. In urban areas, particularly in Middlesex, some of the justices were unscrupulous and corrupt,

[1] An officer of dignity, but with few duties, appointed by the Crown.

with the result that they earned the appellation of 'trading justices'.

Problems resulting from the Industrial Revolution

The Industrial Revolution of the late eighteenth and early nineteenth centuries was marked by the rapid growth of factories and of new large towns. The conversion of Britain from a country which was largely agrarian in character to a great industrial power created new problems with which the eighteenth-century system of local government was totally unfitted to cope. The rapid increase in population and the concentration of population around the newly established factories and coalmines in Yorkshire, Lancashire and the Midlands gave rise to serious administrative difficulties. A system of local government which was intended to deal with rural areas containing scattered populations and which depended on unpaid amateur parish officers to do its work could hardly be expected to contend with the problems to be solved in congested industrial areas—the disposal of great quantities of refuse and sewage, the prevention of disease and of river pollution, the abolition of slums, the suppression of organised crime and the dispersal of clamorous mobs at disorderly vestry meetings.

Even before the advent of the Industrial Revolution it had been the policy of Parliament to establish by local Acts bodies of trustees or commissioners to administer special services in a locality. These *ad hoc* authorities, as they are now called, consisted usually of owners of freehold property above a specified value or of persons named in the Act, serving for life and filling vacancies by co-option. Thus, throughout the eighteenth and early nineteenth centuries statutory bodies known as incorporated guardians of the poor were set up in various parts of the country to relieve the destitute. With the growth of trade and the development of the stagecoach, turnpike trusts were established by local Acts throughout the same period to take over the repair of stretches of road, and from 1748 onwards improvement commissioners were by the same means set up in many urban areas to deal with the paving, lighting and cleansing of the streets. The creation of these *ad hoc* local authorities, particularly turnpike trustees and improvement commissioners, received a strong impetus towards the end of the eighteenth century, when the problems arising from the Industrial Revolution had become manifest. In order to prevent a complete breakdown of local government in some of the new industrial areas, it became necessary to establish these *ad hoc* bodies in greater numbers.

The reform of the poor law and of the municipal corporations

The Reform Act of 1832, which widened the parliamentary franchise and remedied many political abuses, may be said to have transferred the government of Britain from the landed aristocracy to the middle classes. It was natural that the passing of the Reform Act should be followed by insistent demands, especially from the Radicals, for the reorganisation of the local government system on a more democratic and efficient basis. The reform of local government was at length effected by the Poor Law Amendment Act, 1834, which dealt with poor relief, and the Municipal Corporations Act, 1835, which reorganised the boroughs.

The reform of the poor law was long overdue. The Napoleonic Wars had imposed a heavy strain on the economic life of the country, which was reflected particularly in higher food prices, and in the spring of 1795 these higher prices resulted in minor food riots in various parts of the country. It became necessary for the county justices from 1795 onwards to supplement the wages of agricultural labourers by poor relief on a fixed scale, based on the price of bread and the size of the recipient's family. One of the main reasons for setting up a Royal Commission of inquiry into the administration of the poor law in 1832 was the increase in expenditure on poor relief resulting largely from the application of this policy of supplementing wages out of the rates. The Government lost no time in giving effect to the recommendations of the Commission, and the Poor Law Amendment Act, 1834, was passed with little opposition. The parish, which since the days of Elizabeth I had been the unit of poor law administration, was replaced by the union or combination of parishes, and the governing body of the union was the elected board of guardians, which was empowered to appoint paid officers to carry out its work. Hitherto local government, including the administration of poor relief, had been left largely to local discretion, but under the Act of 1834 a strong central body (the Poor Law Commissioners) was set up with wide powers of control over the local boards of guardians. By widening the area of administration and imposing on local authorities a strong measure of central control, it was hoped to effect substantial economies in poor law administration, and this objective was to some extent achieved within the next few years.

Whilst the Royal Commission to inquire into the poor law was engaged in preparing its report, another Royal Commission was appointed to investigate the affairs of the boroughs. Most of these municipalities owed their existence to charters granted between the reign of Henry VIII and the Revolution of 1688. The most common privileges possessed by a borough were the right to return representatives to the House of Commons, the right to hold a market and to levy tolls on traders, and, above all, the right to hold its own courts. The administration of justice was a most valuable jurisdiction because it carried with it immunity from attendance at courts outside the borough, the settlement of cases by the judicial officers of the borough and, more important still, the retention of court fees and fines. In the majority of the boroughs the members of the governing body served for life, and vacancies were filled by co-option. Very few, if any, of the boroughs could be considered municipal democracies in the modern sense. Catholics,

Dissenters and Whigs were excluded from membership of the governing bodies, most of which were Tory character in and strongly partisan in religion and politics, and the same partiality was shown in the administration of municipal charities.

The borough oligarchies concerned themselves chiefly with the administration of justice and the municipal charities and with the management of the corporate property. The main functions of local government—i.e. the relief of the poor, the repair of the roads and the protection of life and property—were exercised by the unpaid parish officers of the individual parishes into which the town was usually divided. From about the middle of the eighteenth century, however, especially in those boroughs where the population was increasing rapidly, some of the most important functions of local government—e.g. paving, lighting, cleansing and policing the streets—were exercised by statutory *ad hoc* authorities, of which the mayor and some of the members of the corporation were usually *ex-officio* members, but these members rarely took any interest in the work of the local statutory bodies.

As most of these municipal corporations were Tory, the Whig Government lost no time in dealing with the question of reform. The Royal Commission, which was appointed in 1833, consisted of nineteen barristers, mainly of Whig sympathies, who toured the country in pairs collecting information. After a survey extending over a period of eighteen months the Commissioners issued their report. Never was a public document more scathing in its condemnation of an established system. The municipalities were represented as hotbeds of venality and partisanship, guilty of the most reckless extravagance in spending their receipts from trust funds and their other resources.

The Municipal Corporations Act, 1835, which followed the publication of the report, gave the municipal vote to the ratepayers. The Act also provided for the election of councillors for a period of three years and for the election by the councillors of aldermen (consisting of one-third of the number of councillors) who would serve for a period of six years. The only important function for which the borough council was made responsible was the control of the borough police, which was to be exercised by the watch committee, consisting of members of the council. The system of election of borough justices of the peace by the municipality was abolished: the Act provided for their appointment by the Crown, as in the counties.

The simplification of the local government structure

From 1835 onwards, as the scope of local government enterprise widened and new problems presented themselves, new *ad hoc* local authorities were created and superimposed on the existing structure. The establishment of local boards of health, highway boards, burial boards, school boards and school attendance committees during this period produced a welter of *ad hoc* authorities with overlapping areas and functions. The finances of each of these authorities were largely unco-ordinated, and no authority by itself was sufficiently important to attract local interest. The structure of local government was aptly described in 1885 as 'a chaos of areas, a chaos of franchises, a chaos of authorities and a chaos of rates'.

The administrative confusion caused by the creation of a multiplicity of *ad hoc* authorities was, however, remedied by a series of enactments, which established *omnibus* local authorities, i.e. local authorities with a wide range of powers and duties, in place of these *ad hoc* bodies. The Local Government Act, 1888, created county councils and county borough councils, and the Local Government Act, 1894, created urban and rural district councils, parish councils and parish meetings. The Education Act, 1902, transferred the responsibility for education from the school boards and school attendance committees to *omnibus* local authorities, and the Local Government Act, 1929, abolished the poor law guardians and transferred their functions to the county councils and county borough councils.

The reform of county government was not accomplished until more than half a century after the reorganisation of the boroughs. From about 1830 onwards there was a strong reaction against the justices of the peace as rulers of the county, and during the period 1830–5 the county justices were deprived of a number of important functions. The unpopularity of the justices was mainly due to the desire for a more representative form of county government. The first of a long series of attempts to substitute an elective authority for the justices was made in 1836, but owing to the poverty and illiteracy of the agricultural labourer it was found very difficult to establish democratic government in rural areas. Eventually, following insistent agitation by Radicals and Trade Unionists, and the passing of the Redistribution Act, 1884, which extended the parliamentary franchise in the counties to householders, it was realised that the reform of county government on representative lines could not be delayed much longer. The Local Government Act, 1888, transferred the administrative functions formerly exercised by the justices of the peace in Quarter Sessions to county councils elected by the ratepayers. Towns with a population exceeding 50 000 were excluded from county control and were created county boroughs with their own elected councils. These county boroughs assumed responsibility for all local government services in their area.

The Local Government Act, 1894, went a stage further in the work of local government reorganisation. Under this Act the smaller towns which had not been created boroughs became known as urban districts, and the area of the county outside the boroughs and urban districts was divided into rural districts. In both urban and rural districts the council was elected by the ratepayers. These urban and rural district councils were at first concerned mainly with sanitary services, but later, as we shall see (Chapters 10 and 11), the scope of their functions was widened considerably. The same

Act, in an effort to infuse more vitality into the parish, which had declined in importance since the loss of its poor law functions in 1834, created parish councils, elected by the ratepayers, and parish meetings—i.e. meetings of all the parish electors.[1]

The Education Act, 1902, which abolished school boards and school attendance committees, and the Local Government Act, 1929, which abolished the boards of guardians, completed the work of local government reorganisation for the time being.

Codification of statute law

The reorganisation of the structure of local government was followed by the simplification of the law relating to local authorities. Until 1930 the enactments relating to the constitution of local authorities and their powers and duties presented a tangled skein of bewildering complexity. This confusion was partly remedied by the passing of the Local Government Act, 1933, which consolidated in one statute the constitution and general powers and duties of local authorities. Statutes passed in the same decade consolidated the law relating to the relief of the poor, town and country planning, children, public health and housing; and the process of consolidation has (with some setbacks) continued since the end of the Second World War. This has culminated in the passing of the Local Government Act, 1972, which repealed the Local Government Act, 1933, reshaped local government on radical lines and redistributed the functions of local authorities.

[1] In the larger parishes there were an elected council and a parish meeting, and in the smaller parishes a parish meeting only.

2 The Structure of Local Government (1894–1972)

Failure to keep pace with changing conditions

The Local Government Acts of 1888 and 1894 settled the
structure of local government for a period of more than
three-quarters of a century. The Act of 1888 created county
councils and county borough councils, and the Act of 1894
created urban district councils, rural district councils,
parish councils and parish meetings. Even in 1888, however,
when the basis of the main structure of local government was
settled, it was realised that from time to time it would be
necessary to alter the structure to conform with social,
economic and demographic developments. The Act of 1888,
therefore, empowered the Local Government Board, which
at that time was the central government department responsible for the supervision of local authorities, to alter the
boundaries of local authorities, to create new authorities and
to combine existing authorities. The Local Government Act,
1929, made provision for a review on similar lines to be
undertaken at ten-yearly intervals. The changes brought
about by these two Acts were, however, far too piecemeal in
character to meet the requirements of a rapidly changing
social and economic situation. From the beginning of the
twentieth century notable improvements took place in
transport and communications, including the advent of the
motor car and later the carriage of heavy loads on the public highway by large commercial vehicles. During the same

period there were large-scale movements of population, particularly in south-east England, where important new industrial areas were established. There was a substantial decline in the rural population and a great increase in the number of people living in urban areas. An increasing number of people adopted the practice of commuting for considerable distances from their homes to their places of work. Moreover, during this period there were important changes in the functions entrusted to local authorities. They assumed responsibility for a number of new functions, including town and country planning, the preservation of civic amenities and the care of children, and greatly increased their powers and duties in relation to education, health, housing, fire protection and the care of the aged and the infirm. On the other hand, shortly after the Second World War, local authorities shed some of their responsibilities, especially in regard to their trading services and their hospitals, to the central government and to public corporations. But despite these social and economic developments and all these changes in functions, no general reorganisation of the local government system was undertaken, except in London. The local government of Greater London was reorganised in 1965 in accordance with the provisions of the London Government Act, 1963.

The structure in tabular form

The table below shows at a glance the structure of local government in England and Wales as it existed before the reorganisation of 1972 and the different types of local authorities. The number of local authorities of each type is given in brackets. (See page 24.)

The central government departments referred to in the table were the departments such as the Department of the Environment, the Home Office and the Department of Education and Science, all of which exercised a measure of control over local authorities. Their functions are dealt with in Chapter 18. The constitution, powers and duties of the Greater London Council, the City of London Corporation and the London borough councils are dealt with in Chapter 20.

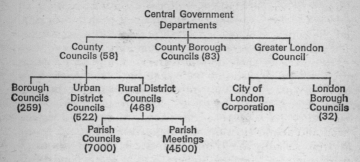

The different kinds of local authorities

County councils—i.e. the councils of administrative counties —were established under the Local Government Act, 1888. England and Wales comprised fifty-two geographical counties or shires and, generally speaking, each of these geographical counties was coterminous with an administrative county, but some of the geographical counties contained two or three administrative counties, each with its own county council. Thus, Sussex comprised two administrative counties (East Sussex and West Sussex), and Yorkshire comprised three administrative counties (West Riding, North Riding and East Riding). In addition, the Isle of Wight was a separate administrative county.

County borough councils were first created under the Local Government Act, 1888 (the Act which established county councils), and a number of new county boroughs were created after that date. County boroughs were normally large towns with a population exceeding 50 000, and the great majority of county boroughs had a population of more than 75 000. They were entirely exempt from the jurisdiction of the county council and were responsible for all the local government functions of their area. A county borough did not form part of an administrative county. The County Borough of Southend-on-Sea, for example, although it was in the geographical county of Essex, was entirely free from the control of the Essex County Council, and the county council had no responsibility for any functions within the area of the county borough.

The whole of each administrative county was divided into county districts, and these county districts were boroughs, urban districts or rural districts, each with its own elected council. Boroughs were sometimes referred to as non-county boroughs, to distinguish them from towns which had acquired county borough status. Borough councils were usually the councils of small or medium-sized towns (many of them of ancient origin) which had been granted a Charter of Incorporation by the Crown. The Charter was an official document which created the borough, defined the boundaries and determined the number of councillors. The functions of a borough council did not differ materially from those of an urban district council, but the conferment of borough status gave the town a position of greater dignity in the local government hierarchy; for whereas a borough council had a mayor, aldermen and councillors, an urban district council consisted of a chairman and councillors only. Some county boroughs and boroughs, generally towns which had been the see of a bishop, had the right to call themselves cities. Although, however, the term *city* might enhance the prestige of a town, it had no local government significance. Both urban and rural district councils were first established under the Local Government Act, 1894. Urban districts, like non-county boroughs, were generally small or medium-sized towns, but rural districts were areas which, as a rule, were much larger and less densely populated than boroughs or urban districts. The rural district grew out of the hundred, which in the Middle Ages was the unit of administration next above the parish.

Rural districts (not urban districts or boroughs) were divided into parishes as units of local administration. Parish councils and parish meetings were first established under the Local Government Act, 1894, but the parish had its origin in the Anglo-Saxon vill or township, which was a centre of population surrounding a church. The larger parishes had elected parish councils, and the smaller parishes were governed by parish meetings, which were meetings of the local government electors of the parish held at least twice a year.

It will be seen from the table on p. 24 and from the explanation following it that if parish councils and meetings, with their limited functions, were taken into consideration as a separate level of administration, local government in England and Wales was partly one-tier, partly two-tier and partly three-tier. In county boroughs, as the council was responsible for all the functions of local government in its area, the structure was one-tier. In boroughs and urban districts the functions were shared with the county council, with the result that the structure in these areas was two-tier. In rural districts the division of responsibility was threefold—i.e. between the county council, the rural district council and the parish council or meeting.

Wide disparities in population and resources

The reader might conclude from the table on p. 24 that a first-tier authority necessarily had a larger population and larger financial resources than a second-tier authority, and that a second-tier authority occupied a similar position in relation to a third-tier authority. He might also assume that there was an approximate similarity between the population and financial resources of each local authority within the same category. The structure of local government, however, contained numerous anomalies and was far removed from this ideal state of affairs. The following are examples of the most patent disparities in England (outside Greater London):

The largest county in population was Lancashire (2 513 400) and the smallest Rutland (29 230).

The largest county borough in population was Birmingham (1 013 420) and the smallest Canterbury (35 530).

The largest non-county borough had a population of 106 610 and the smallest 1580.

The largest urban district had a population of 129 900 and the smallest 1700.

The largest rural district had a population of 102 670 and the smallest 1470.

The disparities in financial resources—i.e. in rateable value and in the product of a rate of 1p in the £—were equally startling.

Rivalry between the boroughs and the counties

Perhaps the chief obstacle to reform was the lack of unanimity of purpose on the part of the different classes of local authorities, an important feature of which was the long-standing rivalry between the counties and the county boroughs. The Local Government Act, 1888, established as county boroughs sixty-one towns, nearly all of which had a population exceeding 50 000. The Act provided for the conferment of county borough status on other boroughs when their population reached this minimum figure, and also for the extension of the boundaries of county boroughs. The procedure for the creation of new county boroughs and for their extension was to be by Provisional Order[1] made by the Local Government Board (from 1919 to 1951 the Ministry of Health). Between 1888 and 1926 a considerable number of boroughs were by Provisional Order promoted to county boroughs, and an even larger number of county boroughs had their boundaries extended. Many of these creations and extensions were vigorously resisted by the county councils, as the award of county borough status to a non-county borough

[1] An Order made by a Minister which conferred no powers until it had been confirmed by an Act of Parliament.

frequently meant that the county in which the borough was situated was deprived of a built-up area with a high rateable value, in consequence of which the county council was forced to continue to maintain its county services, including its main roads, with a reduced revenue. For this reason the county council concerned often looked upon the grant of county borough status to a non-county borough as a major surgical operation from which the patient (the county) could never fully recover. In deference to the demands of the counties it was provided by the Local Government (County Boroughs and Adjustments) Act, 1926, that in future a county borough could be created only by Act of Parliament. By the same Act, the minimum population was raised from 50 000 to 75 000. The conflict between the counties on the one hand and the boroughs and county boroughs on the other still continued, however, and was frequently the subject of prolonged and costly contests in Parliament.

Disagreement between the various types of local authorities was not confined to antagonism between the counties and the boroughs and county boroughs. Urban and rural district councils consistently opposed encroachments by county borough authorities who wished to extend their boundaries at the expense of urban or rural districts, and strongly urged that county councils should delegate as many functions as possible to county districts. County councils, however, showed some reluctance to large-scale delegation of their functions to second-tier authorities.

The Local Government Boundary Commission

In an attempt to resolve these differences of opinion and to keep the structure of local government under constant review, the Local Government Boundary Commission Act 1945, provided for the establishment of a Local Government Boundary Commission. This Commission, which was intended to be permanent, was given wide powers, including the alteration of local government boundaries, the creation of new local authorities, the promotion of boroughs to county boroughs and the demotion of county boroughs. Only boroughs with a population of not less than 100 000 could, under the Act, apply for county borough status, and county boroughs with a population exceeding 60 000 could not be reduced in status. London was excluded from the purview of the Commission, and no part of the County of Middlesex could be constituted a county borough. In its Report for the year 1946 the Commission published statistics showing the extremes in size and population of local government areas of the same designation, but no positive recommendations of major importance were made. By the time the Commission had issued its Report for 1947, however, its members and officers had found time to review the situation. They reached the conclusion that the boundaries of local authorities were inextricably bound up with their functions and that, as the Commission had no jurisdiction over functions, it was useless to formulate proposals dealing with boundaries only. The Commission's Report for 1947, therefore, contained comprehensive proposals not only for the reform of the local government structure but also for the redistribution of local government functions. Some of these proposals required legislation to bring them into operation.

In determining the size of the unit in relation to any given service, the object of the Commission was to make the area of administration as small as was compatible with securing an efficient service. In adopting this principle the Commission took the view that the preservation of local interest was of paramount importance. The report proposed that the smaller counties should be combined to form more effective units of administration and that the larger counties should be divided into two or more counties with the object of securing a population of 200 000 to 1 000 000 in each county. Existing county boroughs with a population exceeding 200 000 were to be renamed 'counties', and a new type of local authority was to be established—a county borough responsible for *most* of the local services in its area. These new county boroughs ('most purpose' authorities) were to be towns with a population of 60 000 to 200 000. The distinction between urban and rural districts was to be abolished.

The recommendations of the Commission were a bold attempt to resolve the sectional differences of the different classes of local authorities and, in particular, to harmonise the conflicting interests of the counties and the boroughs. But these recommendations did not meet with a favourable response from local authorities and would have required fresh legislation, which the Government was not prepared to introduce. Instead of adopting the Commission's proposals, the Government decided to abolish the Local Government Boundary Commission and to repeal the Act of 1945 under which it was set up. This policy was implemented by the Local Government Boundary Commission (Dissolution) Act, 1949, with the result that the problems of local government which the Commission had endeavoured to solve were left unsolved, and the reform of local government was left in abeyance.

The 'freezing' of local government

For a whole decade after the dissolution of the Local Government Boundary Commission the existing local government structure was virtually 'frozen'. Boroughs were free to promote private Bills to become county boroughs, but when these Bills were put forward they were successfully resisted by the Government. In 1950, for example, Ilford and Luton promoted Bills to secure county borough status, and the case for both these towns was presented with cogency and persuasiveness by their sponsors. The Minister of Health, however, though not unsympathetic to the aspirations of these two authorities, rejected their applications, arguing that major changes of this character could not be allowed to be made piecemeal but must await a general reform of the local government system.

Proposals for regional local government

Whilst the Local Government Boundary Commission was engaged in the unenviable task of reviewing the local government structure and in issuing its reports, local authorities were being deprived of many important functions. During the years 1946–8 the management of hospitals, the supply of gas and electricity, the maintenance of numerous main roads and the responsibility for valuation for rating were all transferred from local authorities to the state or to public corporations. It is true that during this period local authorities acquired new powers and duties— e.g. under the Town and County Planning Act, 1947, and functions relating to entertainments under the Local Government Act, 1948—but they were regarded as inadequate compensation for the serious losses sustained. It was contended by local government well-wishers that, if municipal atrophy was to be averted and local government was to maintain its vigour and energy, a radical reform of the outworn structure was imperative. Although there was no general agreement on how the system should be reshaped, a movement in favour of the reform of local government on a regional basis gathered momentum. The exponents of regionalism argued that the only way to check this tendency to transfer functions from local to central government, and to save local government from extinction, was to institute a scheme of regionalism. They envisaged the division of England and Wales into twelve or more large areas, each with its own elected regional council. The regional authority was to be responsible for some of the more important local government services, particularly for services such as planning, transport and technical education, which, it was claimed, required large areas for their efficient administration. Within the region there were to be subordinate local authorities, either on a two-tier or three-tier basis, sharing the remaining local government functions.

Whether local government was to be recast on a regional

basis, or on the basis recommended by the Local Government Boundary Commission, or in accordance with some other scheme of reform, an alteration in the framework appeared to be a matter of urgent necessity. There was little doubt that the limitations of the existing structure, which had remained substantially unaltered since 1894, rendered it difficult for local authorities to attain maximum administrative efficiency, and that legislation to end the impasse could not be long delayed.

The Local Government Act, 1958

In April 1954, the Minister of Housing and Local Government announced his intention of making a statement of policy on the subject of local government reform in the next parliamentary session, and the Government's proposals were set out in a White Paper, which was issued in July 1956. The substance of these proposals was later embodied in the Local Government Act, 1958.

Part II of the Act, which dealt with the reviews of local government in England and Wales, bore a strong resemblance to the Local Government (Boundary Commission) Act, 1945. Two Local Government Commissions, one for England and one for Wales, were established to review the areas of counties and county boroughs and what were described as 'Special Review Areas'. These 'Special Review Areas' were Tyneside, West Yorkshire, Merseyside, Southeast Lancashire and the West Midlands. Areas such as these were sometimes known as 'conurbations'—i.e. groups of neighbouring towns which had grown into continuous built-up areas.

The two Commissions had no jurisdiction over the metropolitan area (Greater London).[1] The Welsh Commission dealt with Wales, in which there were no 'Special Review Areas', and the English Commission dealt in different ways

---

[1] The metropolitan area will be dealt with separately. See Chapter 20.

with the 'Special Review Areas' and the remainder of England, except the metropolitan area.

In their reviews of the counties and county boroughs and of the 'Special Review Areas' the Commissioners were empowered to make proposals for the amalgamation, alteration or abolition of existing counties and county boroughs, and for the establishment of new counties and county boroughs. A population figure of 100 000 was normally regarded as the minimum required for promotion to county borough status. In 'Special Review Areas' the Commissioners were, in addition, empowered to make proposals for the amalgamation, alteration, creation or abolition of county districts, but they had no power to deprive non-county boroughs of their status. In carrying out their reviews the Commissioners were required to consult all the local authorities concerned, and in cases where objections were raised local inquiries had to be held. The Commissioners were then required to submit their proposals to the Minister of Housing and Local Government, and they were to become effective when they had been approved by Parliament.

The English Commission, in issuing proposals covering the greater part of the country, including the 'Special Review Areas', dealt with each area with due regard to its individual problems and its special requirements, and county councils submitted proposals for internal county reviews, involving changes in the status and boundaries of county districts and parishes. The Government accepted some of these proposals, but the changes envisaged in the Local Government Act, 1958, although extensive in their scope, were designed to modify rather than to reshape the existing structure. A fundamental alteration of the framework could have been justified only if it had shown itself to be incapable of meeting current needs. In the White Paper which was issued in July 1956, the Government made it clear that it saw no case for making radical changes in the structure of local government, as it had, on the whole, shown itself capable of adaptation to changing social and economic conditions. In course of time, however, recognition of the need for a more radical approach to the reform of the local government system gained increasing support. Although by 1966 considerable progress had been made in implementing the proposals of the English Commission, their limited terms of reference, which had resulted in piecemeal changes, had precluded consideration of a major rationalisation of the structure of local government (possibly on a regional basis) and the redistribution of functions. Accordingly, in February 1966, the Government announced the establishment of a Royal Commission on Local Government in England to consider the question anew, and the Local Government Commissions for England and Wales were dissolved before they had completed their work.

Local government in Wales

Instead of setting up a Royal Commission for Wales, as they had done for England and for Scotland, the Government issued a White Paper on Local Government in Wales (July 1967). Its recommendations were based on the work of the Local Government Commission for Wales and on an inter-departmental working party set up by the Secretary of State for Wales in 1965. The White Paper proposed the substitution of six new administrative counties for the existing thirteen counties, a substantial reduction in the number of county districts, the demotion of the County Borough of Merthyr Tydfil to non-county borough status, and the retention of Cardiff, Newport and Swansea as county boroughs with revised boundaries. It was also recommended in the White Paper that a Welsh Council, whose members would be appointed by the Secretary of State, should be established. A Welsh Council was set up, but the other proposals received further consideration in the light of the Report of the Royal Commission on Local Government in England.

The Royal Commission on Local Government in England

The Commission of eleven members, under the chairmanship of Lord Redcliffe-Maud, was set up on 31 May 1966 'to consider the structure of local government in England, outside Greater London, in relation to its existing functions; and to make recommendations for authorities and boundaries, and for functions and their division, having regard to the size and character of areas in which these can be most effectively exercised and the need to sustain a viable system of democracy'. Their report was issued in June 1969.

After studying the evidence of 2000 witnesses, including evidence given by Government departments, associations of local authorities, chambers of commerce, trade unions and other interested bodies, the Commission recommended that England (outside London, which was not within its terms of reference as it had already been dealt with under the London Government Act, 1963) should be divided into sixty-one new local government areas, each covering town and country, grouped in eight provinces. In fifty-eight of these local government areas, single authorities (unitary authorities) should be made responsible for all local government services. In the three very large and densely populated areas around Birmingham, Liverpool and Manchester, responsibility for services should be divided between a metropolitan authority, whose key functions would be planning, transportation and major development, and a number of metropolitan district authorities, whose main functions would be education, the personal social services, health and housing. There would be twenty metropolitan districts in all—seven in the Birmingham area, four in the Liverpool area and nine in the Manchester area. The Commission felt that it would not be practicable to create unitary authorities in these three areas as the areas required for transportation, planning and major development would be too large for the personal services.

The sixty-one new local government areas were to be grouped, together with Greater London, in eight provinces, each with its own provincial council. Provincial councils would be elected by the authorities for the unitary and metropolitan areas (including in the south-east the Greater London authorities), but would also include co-opted members. These councils would determine the provincial strategy and planning framework within which the main authorities would operate.

Within the fifty-eight unitary areas, and wherever they were wanted within the three metropolitan areas, local councils would be elected to represent and communicate the wishes of cities, towns and villages in all matters of special concern to the inhabitants. They would have the right to be consulted on matters of local interest and would be given the opportunity of participating in the administration of some of the local services.

The Commission justified the radical and far-reaching nature of their recommendations and the complete replacement of the existing single-tier, two-tier and three-tier system by a predominantly unitary system on the ground that local government, which had undergone no major structural change for three-quarters of a century, had failed to match the pattern of life and work in modern England; and that it was impossible to plan development and transportation properly whilst England was divided between county boroughs and counties, separating town from country. In the view of the Commission, the division of services within each county between the county council and the councils of county districts—i.e. the councils of non-county boroughs and urban and rural districts—and the small size of many local authorities, which had prevented them from employing highly qualified manpower and modern technical equipment, were basic faults, detrimental to the efficient working of local government. Only by reducing the number of local authorities and by revitalising the whole system would local government be able to

survive in face of the encroachments of centralised bureaucracy. The increased size of the new authorities would make
it reasonable to consider bringing the national health
service, including the hospitals, within the framework of
local government.

The members of the Commission were by no means
unanimous in their recommendations. The report was,
however, signed by ten of the Commission's eleven members. The eleventh, Mr Derek Senior, published his own
memorandum of dissent, in which he recommended the
establishment of a predominantly two-tier system of local
government, comprising thirty-five directly elected regional
authorities, which would be responsible for the major
services, including planning, transportation, sewerage,
refuse disposal, water supply, police and education, and
148 directly elected district authorities to administer the
personal social services, excluding education. In four areas
the same authority would exercise both regional and district
responsibilities. These proposals were broadly in line with
the evidence given to the Commission by the Ministry of
Housing and Local Government and by a number of other
Government departments. Mr Senior also proposed that
there should be directly elected common councils at 'grass
roots' level, representing existing parishes and towns or
parts of towns small enough to have a real feeling of community. In addition, he advocated the establishment of five
appointed provincial councils with members nominated
mainly by the regional authorities within their areas. Three
of the members of the Commission disagreed with the
number of unitary authorities proposed. Two of them, Sir
Francis Hill and Mr R. C. Wallis, thought that there should
by sixty-three. The third, Mr Jack Longland, thought that
there should be forty-seven, and that there should be sixteen
metropolitan districts instead of twenty.

Mr Wilson's Labour Government accepted in principle
the main recommendation of the report and, after consulting
the local authority associations, published in February

1970 a White Paper which broadly approved the structure
proposed by the Royal Commission. But the White Paper
differed in some respects from the Royal Commission's
report. There were, for example, to be two additional
metropolitan authorities (Hampshire and West Yorkshire).
making a total of five instead of the three metropolitan
authorities proposed by the Royal Commission, and there
was to be a change in the distribution of functions in two-
tier areas. In June 1970, however, the Labour Government
was replaced by a Conservative administration. The
Conservative Party had pledged themselves to introduce a
system of two-tier local government throughout the country,
with the result that the mainly unitary concept of local
government structure contained in the Royal Commission's
report was rejected. The Conservative White Paper
(February 1971) accepted the concept of metropolitan
areas, excluded Labour's proposal for a South Hampshire
metropolitan area, and increased the total to six by proposing South Yorkshire and Tyne/Wear. Views were invited on
these proposals, and consideration was given to alternative
suggestions. A Bill was introduced in the parliamentary
session of 1971–2, and the substance of the Conservative
White Paper was enacted in the Local Government Act,
1972. Perhaps the most important change from the White
Paper proposals was the creation of a new county of
Humberside, covering the East Riding and Hull and the
South Humberside area of Lincolnshire with Grimsby and
Scunthorpe. The new county and district councils were
elected in 1973, and the new authorities took over their full
functions on 1 April 1974. Thus, after many years of
conflict and dissension, the framework of local government
was settled on lines which, it is hoped, will reflect the pattern
of life in modern society.

Although the structure of local government has undergone a fundamental transformation, many of the ancient
boundaries have been retained. Most of the new county
authorities (with the exception of the new metropolitan

counties) either broadly cover the same areas as the former geographical or administrative counties, or are combinations of two or more such counties. If the proposals made by the Royal Commission on Local Government in 1969 (the Redcliffe-Maud Report) had been accepted and put into operation, the unitary system envisaged in that report would have shown scant respect for former boundaries and would have resulted in structural alterations of an even more sweeping and radical nature than those contained in the Local Government Act, 1972.

3 Local Government Reorganisation

The scope of the Local Government Act, 1972

The Local Government Act, 1972, made provision for the radical reshaping of the structure of local government and for the creation of new local authorities in England and Wales in place of those which ceased to exist. These new local authorities were elected in 1973 and assumed their full powers on 1 April 1974. In round figures, there was a reduction in the number of major local authorities from 1400 to 450. The Act, however, provided not only for the complete reform of the structure of local government but also for important changes in the distribution of the functions of local authorities and in various other matters, such as elections and membership, financial administration, audit, loans, the committee system, the admission of the press to committee meetings and the appointment of staff. The Local Government Act, 1933, which had previously been the main source of information on the constitution and general powers and duties of local authorities, was repealed in its entirety and replaced by the Act of 1972. The provisions of the London Government Act, 1963, relating to the constitution of local authorities in Greater London have, with some modification, been incorporated in the new Act, but there has been no alteration in the structure of local government in London. This chapter will deal mainly with the changes in structure, leaving the other changes to be dealt with in subsequent chapters.

The new local government structure in England

A tabular statement of the new local government structure in England showing the different types of local authorities and the number of authorities in each type is given below, and an explanation of the place occupied by each category of local authority is contained in succeeding paragraphs:

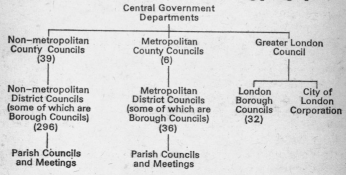

The whole of England (outside Greater London) is divided into forty-five counties, six of which are metropolitan counties, covering the areas of 'conurbations', i.e. areas with a high density of population and mainly urban in character. The remaining thirty-nine counties are non-metropolitan counties. Each county, whether it is metropolitan or non-metropolitan, has its elected county council. Counties are divided into districts, and those in metropolitan counties are called metropolitan districts. Each district, whether it is metropolitan or non-metropolitan, has its elected district council. Some districts are divided into parishes, and the larger parishes have an elected parish council and a parish meeting, whilst the smaller parishes may have only a parish meeting, which is an assembly of the local government electors of the parish.

In an ideal system of local government the population of
each local government area in the same class would show
no marked differences, and one would expect the population of any county to be greater than that of any district.
This was not so, however, before the 1973 reorganisation,
and regrettably it has not been possible to devise a new system which is free from a large number of patent disparities.
Geographical considerations, road and rail communications,
social amenities, community of interest and perhaps respect
for tradition and ancient boundaries, as well as population,
are matters of some significance in the determination of
county and district boundaries. For reasons of practicability,
therefore, and despite intentions to the contrary, the new
structure contains numerous anomalies. Thus, Bristol, the
largest non-metropolitan district, has a population of
425 000, whilst the population of the County of the Isle of
Wight is only 109 000. The population of Bristol is twice
that of many metropolitan districts, which have far wider
powers and duties. The largest non-metropolitan county
has a population of about thirteen times the smallest non-
metropolitan county. The largest district has about fifty
times the population of the smallest. Fourteen districts have
a population of less than 40 000, and the question arises
whether their population and financial resources are sufficient to enable them to discharge their functions with
administrative efficiency. The creation of larger authorities
for these areas, however, might have resulted in the district
councils concerned becoming too remote from the electorate.
Fourteen of the thirty-six metropolitan districts have a
population of less than 250 000, six are under 200 000, and
doubts have been expressed whether these authorities are
large enough to tackle major urban problems.

The county

Most of the names of the thirty-nine non-metropolitan
counties are reminiscent of the Anglo-Saxon shires or of

administrative counties in existence before the reorganisation. Many of them, in fact, embrace the same area as the former administrative county with the addition of one or more of the former county boroughs, which were autonomous local authorities independent of the county council. Thus, the new county of Essex consists of the former administrative county with the addition of the county borough of Southend-on-Sea, and the new county of Devon consists of the former administrative county with the addition of the county boroughs of Exeter, Plymouth and Torbay. Some of the new counties are combinations of two former administrative counties with or without the addition of a county borough. Cambridgeshire, for example, comprises the former administrative counties of Cambridgeshire and Isle of Ely and Huntingdon and Peterborough; and Leicestershire comprises the former administrative counties of Leicestershire and Rutland and the county borough of Leicester.

In forming the new non-metropolitan administrative counties an attempt has been made to marry town and country and to establish areas which are not exclusively rural or urban in character. On the other hand, the six metropolitan counties—Greater Manchester, Merseyside, South Yorkshire, West Yorkshire, Tyne & Wear and West Midlands—are essentially urban in character, comprising the most densely populated areas in the country outside Greater London. It would have been impracticable in these areas to have established local authorities with a balance of town and country. The two-tier pattern of local government in these six areas is somewhat similar to that of Greater London.

The district

All counties in England are divided into districts, and the district is the second tier, the county being the first tier. Those districts which are in the six metropolitan counties are metropolitan districts, and those in the thirty-nine non-metropolitan counties are non-metropolitan districts. The areas of the thirty-six metropolitan districts are set out in the Local Government Act, 1972, but the 296 non-metropolitan districts in England were defined by order of the Secretary of State for the Environment, acting on the advice of the Local Government Boundary Commission for England.[1] Generally speaking, metropolitan districts have a much larger population than non-metropolitan districts, and their councils have much greater financial resources and more extensive powers and duties.

The borough

The Local Government Act, 1972, devoted considerable ingenuity to the preservation of the ceremonial privileges of ancient boroughs. If the former borough or city coincided exactly or approximately with the new district (whether metropolitan or non-metropolitan), the district council was empowered to petition the Crown for a charter conferring borough status. A petition could not be presented unless a resolution of the district council had been passed by a majority of at least two-thirds of the members voting at a specially convened meeting for this purpose. The Queen, acting on the advice of the Privy Council, to which the petition was referred, could grant or refuse a charter. If a charter was granted, the district became a borough, its council became a borough council, and the title of the chairman and the vice-chairman were changed to mayor and deputy mayor respectively. The change in status from district to borough, however, was purely ceremonial, and the functions of a borough council are no different from those of the former district council which it replaced. A large number of districts have, in fact, applied for and been granted borough status. The new district authorities were also allowed to petition the Crown for the retention of the

[1] See p. 48.

right to call themselves cities and for the mayor to be lord mayor.

The parish

The parishes in rural districts which existed in England before the Local Government Act, 1972, continued as parishes after the reorganisation. In rural areas, therefore, there is an elected parish council with a parish meeting in the larger parishes and a parish meeting only—i.e. an assembly of all the local government electors of the parish who choose to attend—in the smaller parishes. If there are 200 or more local government electors in the parish, there must be a parish council and a parish meeting. In the smaller parishes, the district council must establish a parish council if the parish meeting passes a resolution to have one, and provided that the number of local government electors is 150 or more. It may at its discretion do so if the number is less.

Town councils

As a result of the recent reorganisation of local government, a large number of small towns which were formerly non-county boroughs or urban districts ceased to exist as separate authorities and became part of a new district. In the original Local Government Bill no provision was made for the continued existence of these towns as separate local authorities, but the Local Government Act, 1972, empowered the Secretary of State for the Environment, on receipt of an application from the borough or district council, and on the advice of the English Local Government Boundary Commission,[1] to designate an existing small borough or urban district, which would otherwise have lost its separate identity, as a parish. These towns now have a parish council of their own with the added dignity of town council, and the chairman is known as the town

[1] See p. 48.

mayor. They have the same powers and duties as other parish councils. About 300 small towns have become 'successor' councils in this way. Members of the former borough councils and urban district councils (including aldermen in the boroughs) have become the 'successor' parish councils. In general, these new 'successor' councils are responsible for areas with a population between 10 000 and 20 000 and less than 20% of the district of which they form part. If a town has a higher proportion than one-fifth of the population of a district, there is less need for a parish council because the town has a considerable proportion of the councillors in its district, so it would be difficult to claim that the absence of a town council would result in the affairs of the town being dealt with by a small number of over-worked district councillors with wider interests.

Reorganisation in Wales

Although no provision was made for the establishment of a Royal Commission on Local Government for Wales, the structure of local government in the Principality has undergone a radical change similar to that which took place in England. Neither the White Paper on Local Government in Wales[1] (July 1967), with its retention of administrative counties and county boroughs, nor the Report of the Royal Commission on Local Government in England (June 1969) could be regarded as an acceptable basis for reform once it had been decided to introduce a two-tier system for England. Accordingly, the Local Government Act, 1972, reformed the structure of local government in Wales on a two-tier basis on the lines of the new English system, except that in Wales there are no metropolitan counties or metropolitan districts and districts are divided not into parishes, as they are in England, but into communities. Unlike England, which is not wholly divided into parishes, a complete system of communities covers the whole of Wales.

[1] See Chapter 2.

The larger communities have elected community councils with community meetings, and the smaller parishes have community meetings only.

The pattern of local government in Wales is, therefore, as follows:

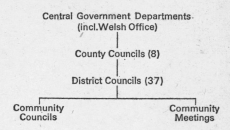

Central Government Departments.
(incl.Welsh Office)

County Councils (8)

District Councils (37)

Community Councils   Community Meetings

Provision was made in the Act for the conferment of borough charters as in England, and, in accordance with directions issued in 1973 by the Secretary of State for Wales, eighty-seven 'successor' community councils have been established (twenty-six based on former boroughs and sixty-one on former urban districts). All former rural parishes have become communities, and where there was previously a parish council there is now a community council. A 'successor' community council may resolve that its area shall have the status of a town, and in such a case the council is the town council and its chairman and vice-chairman are called the town mayor and town deputy mayor respectively.

Alteration of areas

In recognition of the principle that local government areas should not remain static but should be responsive to the facts of growth and change in our society, provision was made in the Local Government Act, 1972, for the new structure to be kept periodically under review. The first

comprehensive review must be undertaken not less than ten
years or more than fifteen years after 1 April 1974, and
thereafter reviews must be undertaken at intervals of not
less than ten or more than fifteen years from the date of the
report on the previous review. For this purpose the Act
made provision for the creation of a Local Government
Boundary Commission for England and a separate Local
Government Boundary Commission for Wales, both
Commissions being advisory. The recommendations of the
English Commission and the Welsh Commission are given
effect by orders of the Secretary of State for the Environment and the Secretary of State for Wales. Orders must be
laid before Parliament for forty days before coming into
operation. The English Commission is required to conduct
comprehensive reviews of all counties, metropolitan districts
and London boroughs and the boundaries of Greater
London. Between these comprehensive reviews the Commission may, on its own initiative, undertake reviews
relating to individual local authorities other than non-
metropolitan districts, and the Commission may also
conduct a review at the request of a local authority. Furthermore, the Commission is under a continuing duty to keep
under review all non-metropolitan districts, and in exercising their powers and duties they may make consequential
alterations of parishes.

Although the Local Government Commission for Wales
is not required to conduct periodical comprehensive reviews, it must keep under review all counties and all
districts. Proposals may be made on the initiative of the
Commission, and there is provision for the making of alterations by the Commission at the request of a local authority.

The Local Government Act, 1972, also contains provisions for the alteration of parishes (in England) and
communities (in Wales). It is the duty of the district council
to keep the whole of its district under constant review and to
consider requests for alterations from parish councils and
parish meetings in England and from community councils

and community meetings in Wales. The district council makes recommendations to the appropriate Local Government Boundary Commission, and the Commission then makes proposals to the Secretary of State. If he accepts these proposals, he gives effect to them by order.

Local authority associations

As a result of the reorganisation of the structure of local government in England and Wales, there have been important changes in the associations of local authorities. Before the reorganisation, the local authority associations consisted of the following bodies:

The County Councils' Association
The Association of Municipal Corporations
The Urban District Councils' Association
The Rural District Councils' Association
The Association of Education Committees
The London Boroughs' Association
The National Association of Local Councils (formerly the National Association of Parish Councils)

These associations, which were officially recognised by the Government, took an active interest in any matters affecting their class of local authority. Perhaps their most important task was to scrutinise carefully any proposals for new legislation affecting the interests of their members and to make representations to the Government department concerned. The Government sometimes consulted the associations before legislation was drafted. The associations, in addition to acting as a watchdog on their members' behalf, provided advice for individual authorities and exchanged views and experience on current problems. The associations also provided representation on a large number of national bodies, including the National Joint Councils, which determine salaries and conditions of service for local government officers. There was also (and still is) an

International Union of Local Authorities, which represents local authorities from over sixty countries and arranges conferences on local government problems for local authorities throughout the free world. Only those countries from the Eastern bloc are ineligible.

When the Local Government Act, 1972, became law, there were strong hopes that local authorities would seize the opportunity to resolve their internal differences and form a single, all-powerful association (or at least a federation) which would speak with one voice. These hopes, however, have not been fulfilled. Perhaps the differences not only in population but also in needs and circumstances create unavoidable differences of viewpoint which preclude the formation of such a body.

The County Councils' Association, the Association of Municipal Corporations, the Urban and Rural District Councils' Associations and the Association of Education Committees have accordingly been replaced by the Association of Metropolitan Authorities, the Association of County Councils and the Association of District Councils. Included in the membership of the Association of Metropolitan Authorities are the following:

The Greater London Council (including the Inner London Education Authority)

The London Borough Councils (also members of the London Boroughs' Association)

The City of London Corporation

The Metropolitan County Councils

The Metropolitan District Councils

The Association of County Councils consists of the non-metropolitan county councils, and the Association of District Councils consists of the non-metropolitan district councils.

4 Elections and Membership

The local government franchise

Before 1918 the local government franchise differed slightly according to the type of local authority whose members were being elected, but in general eligibility to vote depended upon the payment of rates. Since the passing of the Representation of the People Act, 1918, however, there has been one franchise for all local authorities; and the existing law concerning local government elections is contained mainly in the Representation of the People Acts, 1949 and 1969.

A person is not entitled to vote in a local government election unless his name is included in the register of electors —i.e. a list of persons qualified to vote, which is prepared once a year by the registration officer, who is normally the town clerk, clerk or chief executive officer of the borough or district. The voter must be a British subject,[1] at least 18 years of age on the day of the poll, and resident in the area. A new register comes into force each year on 16 February, and the qualifying date is the preceding 10 October. Persons subject to legal incapacity—e.g. persons who are mentally disordered and persons in prison—are not entitled to vote. Peers are entitled to be registered as local government electors, but not as parliamentary electors. For many years there was doubt about the registration

[1] Or a citizen of the Republic of Ireland.

position of students at universities, polytechnics, etc., who normally spend six to eight months a year in their college town and the remainder of the time in their home town. However, a judgment of the Court of Appeal after the 1970 General Election clarified the situation by allowing students to register in their college town even if they were already registered in their home town. They can, of course, cast only one vote.

The Representation of the People Act, 1969, provided for the lowering of the voting age from 21 to 18 in both local government and parliamentary elections. Broadly speaking, therefore, there is now universal suffrage, with equal qualifications for men and women over the age of 18, in both local government and parliamentary elections.

A local government elector who is registered in a parish which has a parish council or a town council is, of course, entitled to vote not only for the election of parish or town councillors but also for district or borough councillors and for county councillors.

Since the passing of the Ballot Act, 1872, the method of voting at both parliamentary and local government elections has been by secret ballot. In this country the elector votes by marking his ballot paper with a cross or crosses, but in the USA and in Holland, in place of paper ballots, voting machines are used. The advantages of these machines are that the votes are automatically counted as they are cast, and polling papers, ballot boxes and time-consuming manual counting are eliminated.

The membership of local authorities

Under the Local Government Act, 1972, membership of a local authority is open to men and women who are British subjects or citizens of the Republic of Ireland aged 21 or over. When the voting age was lowered to 18, the opportunity was not taken to apply the same minimum age to membership. It is still necessary, therefore, for a councillor or an alderman to be at least 21 years of age on the day of nomination and the day of the poll, if there is one. The Speakers' Conference on Electoral Law (an all-party committee of MPs) is, however, now considering the question of whether the age at which a person can become a member of a local authority should be lowered.

In addition to being over the age of 21, a candidate for election must satisfy at least one of the following five requirements both at the date of nomination and, if there is a poll, on the day of the election; he must:

1 be a local government elector and continue to be a local government elector for the area of the authority; or
2 have occupied as owner or tenant land or premises in that area during the whole of the preceding twelve months; or
3 have his principal or only place of work in that area during the whole of the preceding twelve months; or
4 have resided in that area during the whole of the preceding twelve months; or
5 in the case of a parish or community council have resided in the area or within three miles of it during the preceding twelve months.

The great majority of members derive their eligibility for membership by satisfying the first requirement—i.e. they are local government electors for the area of the authority.

All elections are now held on the same day—on the first Thursday in May or a day chosen by the Home Secretary.

Councillors for all local authorities (including those in London) are elected for a period of four years, but members of non-metropolitan district councils started with two three-year terms (i.e. elections in 1973 and 1976) before reaching the standard four-year term in 1979, and similar arrangements apply to parish councillors before going over to their normal four-year term. All members of county councils, parish councils, the Greater London Council and London borough councils retire together at the end of their four-year term of office. In the case of metropolitan district councils, however, there is a special arrangement for one-third of the council to retire at a time—i.e. one-third retire every year, except in a year in which there is an election for the county council. The effect of this arrangement is that there will be district council elections in three consecutive years, followed by a year in which there will be no district council election but in which an election will be held for the county council. Non-metropolitan district councils have the right to choose between simultaneous retirement and a system of retirement by thirds.

The area of the county is divided into electoral divisions, each of which returns one county councillor, and the area of each district is divided into wards. In metropolitan districts, where the councillors retire by thirds, each ward returns a number of councillors which is divisible by three. In non-metropolitan districts wards return either one councillor or a number of councillors divisible by three.

When a casual vacancy occurs in the membership of a local authority—e.g. on account of the death or resignation of a member, or the failure of a member to attend meetings for six months—a by-election is held to fill the vacancy. But when a casual vacancy occurs in the final six months of a member's term of office, that vacancy remains unfilled until the next general election of councillors. Casual vacancies on parish and community councils are normally filled by co-option—i.e. a person is chosen by the council itself (not by the electorate).

The chairman of a county council or district council, who presides at meetings of the council, is elected for a period of one year by the councillors and must already be a councillor. A vice-chairman is appointed by the council from members of the council to act in the chairman's absence. The council is empowered to pay reasonable allowances to its chairman and vice-chairman for defraying their expenses of office. The chairman and vice-chairman of a borough or town council are in a similar position, except that they are known as the mayor and the deputy mayor, or the town mayor and the town deputy mayor. The mayor of a borough or a town occupies a position of great dignity in the locality and represents the borough or town on ceremonial occasions. The chairman of a parish council is elected from among the members, and he, too, may be paid a reasonable allowance. The appointment of a vice-chairman, however, is not obligatory, and the parish council cannot pay him an allowance.

Aldermen

It will be seen that nearly all members of local authorities outside Greater London are now directly elected by the local government electors, but before the coming into operation of the Local Government Act, 1972, this was not so. The chairman of a county, district or parish council and the mayor of a borough or county borough could be chosen from outside the council. In counties and boroughs and in county boroughs the principle of indirect election was extended to aldermen. The aldermanic principle was first introduced by the Municipal Corporations Act, 1835, to provide stability to borough councils, and the principle was extended to county councils and county borough councils by the Local Government Act, 1888. The proportion of aldermen (except in London) was one third of the number of elected councillors, and they held office for a period of six years (instead of the three-year period for councillors), half the aldermen retiring every three years. They were elected by the councillors from the councillors or from persons eligible for election as councillors. The powers and duties of aldermen did not differ from those of councillors. It was sometimes contended that the election of aldermen was undemocratic, but the justification for the method of their selection was that they had been chosen by persons in whom the electorate had shown its confidence. The aldermanic principle was further justified on the ground that it gave an opportunity to men and women of mature judgment and ripe experience who were anxious to avoid the controversy and turmoil sometimes associated with an election to render useful public service. There was also the advantage under the aldermanic system that continuity of administration was ensured by the retention in office of aldermen for a period of six years. However, the Maud Committee on the Management of Local Government in England and Wales, which issued its main report in 1967, recommended that the aldermanic system should be abolished, and this recommendation was endorsed by the Royal Commission on Local Government (1969). The Local Government Act, 1972, accordingly abolished aldermen, except in Greater London where the GLC aldermen, who were elected in 1973, will continue until 1977, and the London borough council aldermen, who were elected in 1974, will continue until 1978.

Provision is made in the Act of 1972 for the conferment by local authorities of the title of honorary alderman on persons who have, in the opinion of the council, rendered eminent services as past members of that council. The recipient of the honour has no right to take part in council business.

Procedure for the election of councillors

The officer responsible for the conduct of elections—e.g. for the arrangements for the provision of polling stations where the votes are recorded, the printing of ballot papers and the counting of the votes—is known as the returning officer. For the elections of county and district councillors, the appointment is made by the council concerned, and the person appointed is normally the clerk, the town clerk or the chief executive officer. For elections of parish and community councils, the district council appoints one of its officers.

A candidate for election to the office of councillor must be duly nominated, and for county and district council elections and for elections to councils in London nominations are required to be in writing, signed by a proposer, seconder and eight other local government electors for the area in question. Nominations for elections to parish and community councils require the signatures of a proposer and seconder only. All questions relating to the validity of nomination papers are decided by the returning officer. Unlike parliamentary elections, in which the candidate is required to pay a deposit of £150, which is forfeited unless he succeeds in obtaining at least one-eighth of the total number of votes cast, no deposit is payable by candidates in local government elections.

Since the coming into operation of the Representation of the People Act, 1969, a candidate in a local government election has been permitted to indicate on his nomination paper the political party to which he belongs, and this information is shown on the ballot paper. Until that time the fiction had been maintained that elections were contests between individuals. This change was introduced because it had become evident that in some local government elections, particularly those for the Greater London Council, where there was sometimes a large number of candidates for an electoral area, voters had been confused when confronted with identical or similar names.

If the number of candidates is not greater than the number of vacant seats, all the candidates are declared by the returning officer to be returned unopposed. If, however, the number of candidates exceeds the number of vacant seats, the returning officer makes the necessary arrangements for the holding of an election. The expenses incurred by the returning officer in the conduct of the election are defrayed by the local authority, but the candidate (or the political party by which he is sponsored) does incur expenses in preparing his election address, displaying posters, hiring halls for meetings, etc. In some areas, before the election, party candidates are invited by their local party organisation to make a contribution towards the election expenses. These expenses are limited by law to £30 with an additional 5p for every six entries in the register; there are reductions in the case of joint candidates, and higher limits for GLC elections. Expenses may not be incurred by the candidate in hiring motor vehicles for the conveyance of electors to the poll, in bribing electors to procure their votes or in providing food or drink. To incur expenses for these purposes would be a corrupt or illegal practice.

The elector is normally required to attend in person at the polling station to record his vote, but arrangements for voting by post are made for certain classes of voters—e.g. blind persons and persons who cannot attend owing to illness or physical incapacity. Service voters are allowed to vote by proxy—i.e. they can nominate a person to vote on their behalf. People working outside the United Kingdom—e.g. seamen, fishermen and other persons abroad on their normal business—may also vote by proxy. Electors who moved to another part of the country shortly before the election are not allowed to vote in their new area, but may apply for a postal vote, and people on holiday are not permitted to vote in the holiday area.

The candidate is entitled to visit the polling stations, and he and his agents appointed by him may be present at the count. The candidate may demand a recount when the voting is close. If the number of votes cast for each of two candidates is exactly equal, the returning officer is required to cast lots to determine which candidate has been elected.

The elected member must, within two months of the date of his election, make a declaration of acceptance of office, and failure to do so has the effect of causing a vacancy.

Disqualifications for election

In order to ensure, as far as possible, that the men and women who serve as members of local authorities are fit to hold office, and that public duty does not conflict with private interest, a number of disqualifications have been prescribed by the legislature. Under the Local Government Act, 1972, a person is disqualified from being elected to membership or from continuing his membership of a local authority in the following circumstances:

1 *Paid office*

Any person who holds paid office or employment (other than that of mayor, deputy mayor, chairman or vice-chairman) with a local authority or any of its committees is disqualified from membership. Were it not for this disqualification, a councillor in the employ of his authority might be tempted to manipulate its policy to his own advantage, but even cleaners, caretakers, groundsmen, persons employed on routine clerical work and part-time staff are disqualified from membership; and there is considerable support for the view, especially from the Trades Union Congress, that a liberalisation of the law on the disqualification of employees would be desirable. The Redcliffe-Maud Committee on conduct in local governments (May 1974) recommended, however, that employees should continue to be legally disqualified for election to their employing authority. Under the Education Act, 1946, teachers employed in schools (including voluntary schools) which are maintained by the council or in assisted schools may not be members of the council, but they may be members of the education committee or the public libraries' committee of the council. An employee of one local authority is, of course, not debarred from membership of another local authority. An employee of a county council, for example, may serve as a member of a district or borough council. Under the Local Government Act, 1972, a person who is a member of a local authority is precluded from being appointed by that authority to any paid office for a year after he has ceased to be a member.

2   *Bankruptcy*

A person who has been adjudged bankrupt or has made a composition with his creditors is disqualified from membership. The disqualification ceases not later than five years from the date of discharge from bankruptcy.

3   *Criminal offences*

A person who has within five years before election or since his election been convicted of any offence and ordered to be imprisoned for a period of three months or more without the option of a fine is disqualified from membership of any local authority.

4   *Corrupt and illegal practices*

Certain practices at elections—e.g. bribery, personation, treating, undue influence and hiring vehicles to convey electors to the poll—are corrupt or illegal practices, which are punishable as criminal offences. These offences involve disqualification from membership of local authorities for varying periods.

5   *Expenditure exceeding £2000 contrary to law*

If, in the course of an audit of a local authority's accounts, a member is found to have incurred or authorised expenditure exceeding £2000 which is contrary to law, the court may by order disqualify that member from being a member of a local authority for a specified period. But for this provision, an impecunious member of a local authority could continue to authorise illegal expenditure with impunity, as any requirement to repay the unlawful expenditure to the local authority would in itself have no deterrent effect.[1]

[1] The Local Government Act, 1933, provided that a person who had within five years before the date of election or since election been surcharged to an amount exceeding £500 by a district auditor, i.e. a Government auditor, was disqualified from membership of any local authority. This provision has been re-enacted in the Local Government Act, 1972, but it will cease to be effective at the end of five years from 31 March 1974.

Pecuniary interest

Prior to the operation of the Local Government Act, 1933, persons interested in a contract with a local authority were disqualified from membership of that authority, but the extension of the scope of local government activity rendered it impracticable to continue this disqualification. The position now is that interest in a contract with a local authority is no longer a disqualification from membership. A builder, for example, is not precluded from accepting a contract to undertake work for a local authority of which he is a member. In place of disqualifications there are provisions which require a member who is financially interested, directly or indirectly, in a contract to disclose his interest, and also which prohibit him from taking any further part in any proceedings of the council or its committees relating to the matter in question. Some local authorities have made standing orders which not only prohibit the member from speaking and voting but also provide for his exclusion from any meeting relating to the matter in question. The provisions in the Local Government Act, 1972, relating to pecuniary interest have made concessions in favour of holders of small numbers of shares in companies, and the Secretary of State for the Environment has granted a general dispensation to members of local authorities who are council tenants, enabling them to speak and vote on general matters concerning council housing, including rents, but not in relation to a house of which the member is himself a tenant.

Following disquieting disclosures of malpractices by a small number of members and officers of local authorities, the Government in October 1973 announced the setting up of a Committee of Inquiry under the chairmanship of Lord Redcliffe-Maud to examine the conduct of both members and officers in situations where there is, or could be, a conflict between their position in local government and their private interests. The Committee's terms of reference also

included an examination of the qualifications and disqualifications for membership of local authorities and their
committees. The Committee recommended in May 1974
that there should be a national code of conduct for councillors; that there should be a statutory register of their
pecuniary interests; and that people working for local
authorities should continue to be disqualified for election
to their employing authority. In the meantime, a number of
local authorities have taken the initiative by establishing a
voluntary public register of the pecuniary interests of
elected members and officers, including details of director-
ships and shareholdings in companies; and there was support from a minority of local authorities for a proposal to
establish a compulsory register, which would be open to
public inspection.

Apathy in local government

In parliamentary general elections, from three-quarters
to four-fifths of the electors exercise their vote, but the proportion of the electors who take the trouble to go to the poll
in local government elections is considerably smaller. In
fact, in normal circumstances, rather less than 40% of the
local government electorate exercise their vote. One
explanation which is sometimes offered for the low percentage of votes cast in local government elections is that so
complete is the confidence reposed by the local government
elector in the reputation of elected members and in the
achievements of local government that he considers there is
no necessity for him to go to the poll. This facile explanation
is, however, scarcely tenable.

Apathy is not confined to the failure of the majority of the
electors to record their votes. In many constituencies,
especially in rural areas, the election of councillors is un-
contested as the number of candidates nominated is equal
to or fewer than the number of vacant seats. Before the 1973
reorganisation of the structure of local government only

about half the seats in county and rural district council elections were contested. Numerous cases could be cited of a candidate being returned unopposed time after time for the same seat.

A large number of suggestions have been made on the methods to be adopted to induce electors to record their votes and generally to stimulate interest in local government. In the USA considerable use has been made of radio in reporting local government activities; some municipalities even own and operate radio stations, and the entire proceedings of council meetings have been televised. In Britain in 1967, when public attention was focused on local government by the *Report of the Maud Committee on the Management of Local Government in England and Wales*, the BBC produced a series of television programmes entitled *Inside Local Government*. In addition, a meeting of a city council has been broadcast, and on several occasions viewers have been offered an opportunity of hearing and seeing the proceedings of a local authority on their television sets. There has also been a number of television programmes of a fictional nature with a background of local government. Although radio and television have from time to time been used as weapons by local authorities in their battle with the electorate against apathy and indifference, attempts to evoke widespread interest in local government have met with little success.

Some local authorities employ public relations officers, and although the valuable work done by these officers is fully recognised by most local authorities there is a natural reluctance in times of financial stringency to undertake any optional service which involves expenditure. The result is that many local authorities do not employ officers exclusively on this type of work, nor do they maintain information centres (where inquiries are answered about the services available in the area), which they are empowered to do under the Local Government Act, 1972. Some local authorities give financial assistance to citizens' advice bureaux, which are voluntary organisations providing advice and information to the public free of charge on a wide variety of matters, including housing.

Among other suggestions designed to develop closer contact between the elector and the local authority are that more local authorities should organise civic weeks, exhibitions and film shows; that local authorities should issue civic news sheets; and that debates, brains trusts and quizzes should be held periodically. One local authority adopted an ingenious publicity device for explaining local government reorganisation by running a competition to find a beauty queen for the new district. She was the first beauty queen to publicise local government reorganisation. Since the coming into operation of the Local Government Act, 1972, members of the press and the public have the right to attend not only meetings of the full council but also meetings of its committees, and it may well be that as a result of this provision a higher proportion of the electorate will take a greater interest in the activities of their local council.

Perhaps the most fruitful method of approach to the problem of apathy in local government is in the education of the young. At least one enterprising local authority conceived the novel idea of establishing a junior city council, whose purpose was to encourage the interest of young people between the ages of 14 and 18 in civic affairs. At present, citizenship, including local government, if taught at all in school, is normally relegated to a subordinate position in the curriculum, and very often it is not treated as a separate subject but is dealt with incidentally as part of another subject. In a democracy with universal suffrage from the age of 18 upwards it is particularly important that citizenship should not be regarded as the Cinderella of school subjects. One reason for the apathy shown by the elector in local government affairs is his lack of knowledge of the rudiments of the local government system. For example, a survey conducted several years after the creation of the Greater London Council showed that about one-third of the Londoners who were questioned thought that the GLC administered the London hospitals. There is little doubt that the placing of citizenship on a footing of equality with other subjects in all secondary schools would lead to a greater awareness of its importance and would encourage electors to participate more actively in both central and local government.

5 The Practical Working of Local Government

Council meetings

In order to deal with the work entrusted to them, local authorities find it necessary to hold periodical meetings. At these meetings matters raised by the officers of the council or by council members are discussed, and decisions are normally reached by a majority of those council members who attend the meeting and cast their votes. Voting is by show of hands.

The Local Government Act, 1972, requires each council to hold an annual meeting and to meet on such other occasions as may be necessary for the transaction of its business. Three clear days' notice must be given of a meeting, and the notice must specify the business to be dealt with. A parish council must meet at least four times a year, but a community council is not required to hold a minimum number of meetings during the year. A parish meeting must assemble at least once a year (twice a year if there is no parish council). Pressure of business, however, renders it necessary for principal councils—i.e. the local authorities in London and county, district and borough councils outside London—to meet at fairly frequent intervals. For many years the Greater London Council adopted the practice of meeting at fortnightly intervals (now three-weekly), and the London boroughs hold council meetings at least every six weeks. Meetings are held at the time fixed by the council. Owing to travelling difficulties, county councils and other local authorities covering wide areas normally hold their meetings in the morning or afternoon, but evening meetings are held in the London boroughs and in some of the urban areas outside London. The Act of 1972 provides that the proceedings of a parish meeting may not commence before 6.00 p.m., and the meeting may not be held in a public house unless no other suitable room is available.

No business may be transacted by a local authority unless a minimum number (quorum) of members is present. For principal councils a quorum is a quarter of the whole number of members of the council, and for parish councils and community councils it is a third. The names of members attending council meetings must be recorded.

Admission of the press and the public to meetings

Under the Public Bodies (Admission to Meetings) Act, 1960, any meeting of a local authority was open to the public, but an authority could by resolution exclude the public whenever publicity would be prejudicial to the public interest by reason of the confidential nature of the business to be transacted or for other special reasons. There was a requirement that at a meeting which was open to the public representatives of newspapers were to be afforded reasonable facilities for reporting the proceedings, and a copy of the agenda had to be supplied to any newspaper which requested it. Included in the bodies to which this Act applied were education committees. The Act gave no right to the public or the press to attend meetings of committees (except the education committee) or subcommittees. Many local authorities, however, wishing to afford the widest publicity to their proceedings and to encourage public participation in local affairs, allowed the press and the public to attend meetings of their committees, and a smaller number of local authorities allowed the press and the public to be present at meetings of subcommittees. The Local

Government Act, 1972, has amended the Act of 1960 by extending to the press and the public the right to attend not only the full meetings of the council but also committee meetings, including meetings of joint committees, but not meetings of subcommittees. But public galleries are still, as a rule, sparsely attended because the proceedings of a local authority are often dull and unintelligible to an elector with little knowledge of the rudiments or the complexities of local government. Normally only a local controversy which arouses widespread interest and strong passions can fill the public gallery.

Standing orders

Under the Local Government Act, 1972, local authorities are empowered to make standing orders. These standing orders are rules made by the local authority regulating its proceedings and internal organisation, including rules relating to such matters as the conduct of meetings, the admission of the public to meetings, the method of appointment to committees, the quorum at committee meetings, the order of business, the placing of council contracts, invitations for competitive tenders, and the appointment of staff. The Government has published a set of model standing orders for the guidance of local authorities.

Inspection of documents

Under the Local Government Act, 1972, the minutes of the proceedings of a local authority are open to inspection by any local government elector. Although this provision applies to proceedings of council meetings, it does not apply to all committee proceedings. If the committee is exercising referred powers and its proceedings have been submitted to the council for approval, the minutes are open to public inspection, but the rule as to the right of inspection does not apparently apply where a committee is exercising delegated powers.[1] Until the coming into operation of the Local Government Act, 1972, a small fee could be charged for inspection, but there is now no charge. Minutes may be recorded in a book or on loose leaves, consecutively numbered.

The committee system

Owing to the large volume of business to be transacted, local authorities find it necessary to entrust some of their functions to committees. The largest councils have more than a hundred members, and on account of their size and the formality of their proceedings it is essential for most of the powers and duties of the council to be dealt with, at any rate in the first instance, by committees of the council rather than by the whole council, each committee concerning itself with one aspect or a number of related aspects of the council's work. Joint committees are sometimes set up by two or more local authorities to provide a service which cannot be conveniently administered within the area of a single local authority. The committee system has been aptly described as the workshop of local government. Under the Local Government Act, 1933, local authorities were empowered to appoint such committees as they thought fit, provided that at least two-thirds of the committee were members of the council. The committees set up under this general power could be either standing committees—i.e. committees of a permanent character, which dealt with a section of the - local authority's administration—or special committees, which were required for only a limited period to deal with a particular matter needing consideration. But some of the most important committees set up by local authorities were those committees which they were compelled to appoint— i.e. the statutory committees. Thus, county councils, county borough councils and the London borough councils were required by law to appoint a health committee and a

[1] See p. 73.

social services committee, and also an education committee, which had to include persons with specialist knowledge and experience; county councils were required to appoint a finance committee; and those county borough councils which were police authorities were required to appoint a watch committee, one-third of whose members were required to be magistrates, to control the county borough police force. All matters relating to the functions for which a statutory committee was appointed had to be referred to the committee, and, except in cases of urgency, the council was precluded from reaching a decision until it had considered the report of the statutory committee.

The Maud Report

The Maud Committee on the Management of Local Government (1967) recommended, in the interests of economy and administrative efficiency, a drastic reduction in the number of committees and subcommittees and in the number of persons serving on each committee. Many local authorities adopted these recommendations. Thus, an authority with, say, fifteen main committees reduced the number to six or seven, and fewer members served on each committee. One of the main objects of this change was to make the work of local government less time-consuming for members. The Maud Committee also proposed that each local authority should establish a management board of from five to nine members, which should formulate the principal objectives of the authority and take the major decisions, with the result that the other committees of the authority would be largely deliberative and advisory bodies with very little power. Although this proposal was not accepted by any major local authority, many authorities set up policy committees with wide powers of overall planning and co-ordination. The Royal Commission on Local Government (1969) recommended that in every main authority there should be a central committee to advise the council on its strategy and priorities, co-ordinate the policies and work of the service committees, and ensure that the best managerial methods were adopted.

Abolition of some statutory committees

One of the recommendations of the Maud Committee (1967) was that local authorities should be relieved of the necessity of appointing specific committees—i.e. statutory committees should be abolished, and the local authority should be free to organise its committee structure to meet its individual requirements. This freedom has, to a certain extent, been conceded by the Local Government Act, 1972, which abolished some but not all of the statutory committees. The most important exceptions are the education committee of a local education authority, the county police committee and the social services committee. The appointment of these committees is still obligatory, but otherwise local authorities have a free hand in the determination of their committee structure. The majority of the members of an education committee must be members of the local education authority, but the committee must include people who have had experience in education and who are acquainted with educational conditions in the area. A social services committee must have at least a majority of its membership consisting of members of the local authority. In practice, the proportion of co-opted members—i.e. those who are not council members—of an education committee or of a social services committee is normally considerably less than a half, and on some of these committees it is only a small minority. Two-thirds of the members of a police committee are county councillors, and the remaining third are magistrates.

The Bains Report

In 1971 the Secretary of State for the Environment and the local authority associations set up a study group on local authority management structures under the chairmanship of Mr M. A. Bains, Clerk of the Kent County Council. The Committee, which consisted of four clerks and two treasurers to local authorities and a company secretary, contained no local authority members. Their recommendations (1972) provided practical advice on management structure for the new local authorities which were shortly to be established. Although their proposal that all statutory committees should be abolished was not accepted, their main recommendations have commanded widespread approval. They recommended that all important matters of policy and finance should be dealt with by a policy and resources committee, which should include opposition members, and that there should be three resources subcommittees—for finance, manpower and land—the members of which should not be drawn solely from the membership of the full committee. Most of the new local authorities have accepted a central policy committee as the basis of their committee structure, and many have set up three resources subcommittees. Although very few councils (if any) have accepted all the Bains proposals, there is no doubt that the report has made a very considerable impact.

The finance committee

The finance committee of a local authority (or the finance subcommittee, if the Bains recommendations are strictly adopted), as the watchdog over the council's income and expenditure, plays a vital part in shaping the council's financial policy. The annual estimates of income and expenditure are prepared for each department of the council by the officers concerned and, after consultation with the council's treasurer or chief financial officer, are submitted by the head of the department to the appropriate spending committee—e.g. the education committee or the housing committee—and subsequently to the finance committee. If there is disagreement between the spending committee and the finance committee, and the matter in dispute cannot be settled by negotiation or compromise, the arbiter in the last resort is the central policy committee or the council itself. In any case, the annual estimates require council approval. In the larger local authorities the position of the chairman of the finance committee in many respects resembles that of the Chancellor of the Exchequer. On 'budget day' he makes a lengthy speech, explaining in some detail the financial problems of the council and perhaps the difficulties involved in improving standards of service and in meeting the cost of all his party's cherished projects, and he asks the council to approve his proposals, including the amount of the rate in the £ to be levied for the ensuing year.

Delegation to committees

The Local Government Act, 1972, empowers local authorities to make arrangements for the discharge of their functions by a committee, a subcommittee, an officer of the local authority or by any other local authority. Any of the council's functions other than the levying of a rate or the raising of a loan may be delegated. The extent to which functions are delegated to committees, however, differs widely from one local authority to another. Some local authorities make full use of delegation: the committee is empowered to decide questions of policy, subject to the requirement that its proceedings are reported periodically to the council. Other local authorities use the power of delegation sparingly: they insist on the committee reporting its proposals to the council before any action is taken. Many local authorities adopt a compromise policy, the committee being given full responsibility, subject to specified powers being reserved to the council. These powers may include such matters as proposals for the establishment of a new service, approval of all contracts above a certain figure and the institution of important legal proceedings. The chairman of a committee (he is sometimes selected by the committee itself) is usually empowered to act on behalf of the committee between meetings in matters of urgency.

Where the volume of work to be dealt with by a committee is large, subcommittees are appointed to attend to sections of the work. If powers are delegated to a committee, the committee may in turn delegate those powers to a subcommittee.

Co-option on committees and subcommittees

Membership of the finance committee on a local authority is limited to members of the council, but in order to secure the full benefit of special knowledge and experience a local authority is empowered under the Local Government Act, 1972, to include in the membership of other committees of the council persons who are not members of the local authority. The proportion of members of a committee (other than a statutory committee) who are not council members may not exceed one-third, but this limit does not apply to subcommittees. The inclusion of these co-opted members on committees and subcommittees is occasionally the subject of controversy. It is sometimes contended that such membership is undemocratic and that co-opted members may impose a financial burden on the electorate without shouldering electoral responsibility. Some councils, especially where party feeling is strong, regard co-option as compensation for candidates who have been unsuccessful in a recent council election, thus giving authority to the very persons who have been rejected by the electorate as council members. The Maud Committee on the Management of Local Government (1967 report) recommended, however, that greater use should be made of co-option. It is interesting to note that co-opted members need not have the qualifications which elected members must possess. As they are not required to be of full age, it would, for example, be in order for schoolchildren under the age of 18 to be co-opted to a road safety committee. Moreover, co-opted members need not have any residential or other association with the area of the local authority concerned.

The relations between officers and committees

Normally a substantial part of the business dealt with by a committee consists of reports prepared by the council's salaried officers. These reports usually contain a lucid summary of the facts relating to the proposal on which the committee are asked to reach a decision, followed by a recommendation (or recommendations) of a responsible officer— e.g. the head of the department. Sometimes a definite course of action is not recommended, but instead the officer in his report outlines as impartially as he can the advantages and disadvantages of the proposal, and asks the committee to decide. Occasionally the officer may put two or more alternative suggestions to the committee for their consideration. It is the committee (or the council where the committee is not acting under delegated powers) who finally decide, and the role of the officer is limited to such advice and guidance as is necessary to enable the committee to reach a decision. The members of the committee are, however, usually amateurs, and they can scarcely avoid placing some reliance on the judgment of the officer, who is usually a person of some experience and frequently of expert knowledge. But the extent to which a committee depends upon officers in reaching a decision depends largely on the type of subject-matter which is being considered. Where the matter under discussion is a delicate human problem, requiring common sense but little or no specialised knowledge, or where it is a controversial matter, likely to arouse strong feelings of passion in the locality, the committee's decision might well be in conflict with the advice proffered by the officer. If, on the other hand, the question under consideration is highly technical in character or one of considerable complexity, the tendency is for the committee to accept the recommendations of the paid expert.

Delegation to officers

It is often said that policy is determined by the council and its committees, whilst administration is the concern of the officers. There are, however, no clear definitions of policy and administration which are generally acceptable, and this was the view adopted in the Maud Committee Report on the Management of Local Government (1967). Administrative detail shades imperceptibly into policy. Thus, both committees and officers acting on behalf of the council under delegated powers may have authority to appoint and promote staff, issue licences, allocate council tenancies, grant mortgages for house purchase and arrange for admission to council homes. Until recently the law did not provide for the delegation of functions to officers, but the Maud Committee (1967) and the Mallaby Committee on the Staffing of Local Government (1967) both recommended that the law should be amended to permit delegation of powers to principal officers, and the Report of the Royal Commission on Local Government (1969) contained a recommendation in similar terms. Under the Town and Country Planning Act, 1968, a local authority was empowered to delegate to any officer the function of determining applications for planning permission, and now, under the Local Government Act, 1972, a local authority may arrange for the discharge of any of their functions by an officer of the authority, except the levying of a rate or the raising of a loan; but even before this legislation was passed, delegation to officers, particularly by the larger local authorities, was quite extensive. This practice not only enables matters to be dealt with more expeditiously but also provides more attractive careers for the officers concerned.

The party system

In most parts of the country, especially in the larger built-up areas, local government is run on party lines. In these areas

candidates for election to membership of the local authority
are chosen by the local political party organisation, and the
party which has a majority on the council uses its majority
to secure the adoption of its policy. The minority, which
functions as the opposition, opposes as a matter of policy all
major proposals introduced by the majority party. Important decisions are sometimes reached in advance of council
and committee meetings by a party caucus, which is a
committee of the political party holding meetings in
private. Today the three main parties in local government
are Conservative, Labour and Liberal, but candidates
are also nominated by the Communists and the Welsh
Nationalists, and by the National Front, an extreme right-
wing organisation. In some areas numbers of 'independent'
members, claiming no party affiliation, obtain seats on
the council, but as the avowed policy of these candidates
is frequently strict economy in local administration and
retrenchment in the social services these 'independents' are
often regarded by the Labour Party as Conservatives in
disguise.

Many of the questions at issue in local government have
little or no relevance to politics, and fortunately it is sometimes possible to reach decisions on these questions in an
atmosphere free from party conflict. There are, however, a
number of contentious matters which seem inevitably to
evoke cogent political argument. Perhaps the most controversial subjects in local government are housing and education. Thus, Conservatives favour the sale of council houses
to council tenants, to which the Labour Party are generally
opposed. Conservatives have consistently upheld the principles embodied in the Housing Finance Act, 1972, which
have antagonised the Labour Party, and in a few Labour-
controlled areas there has been open defiance of the provisions of this Act, the contention being that the 'fair rents'
which the Act applied to council tenants are not, in fact,
fair. In education there is some measure of agreement between the parties, but in the field of secondary education the

Labour Party is fully committed to the establishment of a system of non-selective comprehensive schools throughout the country, to the exclusion of all other secondary schools; whilst the Conservatives, as a general rule, prefer a selective system, which would involve the retention of at least some of the grammar schools. In public works the Conservatives support the employment of private contractors, whilst Labour prefer direct works—i.e. building construction and repairs carried out not by independent contractors on a profit basis but by employees of the local authority.

The merits and demerits of the party system in local government have been argued at length with cogency in the press and elsewhere. The party system, it is claimed, arouses electoral interest. The financial support of the party machine is, for a candidate without means, the only way of contesting an election, and if such support were lacking the number of members returned unopposed would be even greater than it is at present. Where the party system is in operation, the dominant party can concentrate its attention on a limited number of selected objectives and carry through its policy by means of the party machine, whereas in a council without political parties, the members, being unorganised, tend to drift and vacillate, thus hampering the formulation of a coherent policy. It is also contended by those who favour party government that it has the further advantage of ensuring stability and continuity in local administration, particularly in those areas where one party assumes control of the council and remains in power for many years. There is little doubt that some of the greatest achievements of local government have been in those areas —e.g. London and Birmingham—where party politics have dominated public life.

The main criticism directed against the party system by its detractors is that the system deprives the individual member of his freedom of conscience. By being more or less compelled to vote with his party on a particular issue, whether or not he is in agreement with party policy, he is required to sacrifice his individual judgment and initiative on the altar of party dogma. Many questions which could be settled amicably in an atmosphere free from political strife produce feelings of rancour and discord when brought into the maelstrom of party politics. The majority party appoints its own nominee to the chairmanship of each committee, and the traditional impartiality associated with the office of chairman is thereby lost. Where party government holds full sway, candidates for election may be confined to those who are members of a political party, with the result that men and women who owe no political allegiance are prevented from rendering beneficial service to their fellow citizens.

In the past, officers of the council have been expected to adopt an objective and impartial approach to their duties and to give loyal service to their employing authority regardless of its political orientation. In 1973, however, the Labour-controlled Greater London Council appointed at the expense of the ratepayers a number of political staff, including an officer at a salary of £3750 a year as personal aid to the GLC leader. The salary of the personal aid to the former Conservative Leader of the Council was paid for out of party funds, and the latter voiced his criticism of the appointment of 'support staff' in the most forthright terms, his contention being that it was 'totally wrong that London's ratepayers should be forced to pay for political commissars'. The GLC staff journal (*London Town*) objected to the appointment with equal vehemence on the ground that 'entry into the public service is not a perquisite to be handed out by victorious politicians. That is what has distinguished County Hall and every other town hall from Tammany Hall.' Whether other councils will follow the example of the GLC in making political appointments remains to be seen.

6 The Work of a Councillor

The newly elected councillor

Most councillors are sponsored by political parties, and in most areas the newly elected councillor will have fought an election in order to obtain his seat on the council. Having successfully survived the excitement and the turmoil normally associated with a local government election, the new councillor will be invited a few days after his election to a meeting of his political group of the council. He may be asked by his colleagues about his special interests, and he will probably be invited to serve on, say, two or three committees of the council to which, it is hoped, he will make a useful contribution. Some new councillors have favourite hobby horses, and others may be strongly imbued with altruistic ideas for the improvement of the locality in which they live. They will doubtless wish to serve on those committees which appear to afford the greatest scope for the furtherance of their pet projects. A new councillor may well be advised by his more senior colleagues to curb his enthusiasm by not making his maiden speech in the council chamber until he has had a few months' experience on the council. Many young members regard local government as a stepping-stone to the House of Commons.

One of the first things that a newly elected councillor (even if he has previously served as a councillor) must do is to sign a declaration of acceptance of office, which, under

Membership of statutory and voluntary bodies

In addition to attending meetings of the council and its committees and subcommittees, and perhaps, in connection with his membership of committees, making visits of inspection to schools, children's homes and old people's homes, and to building sites in connection with planning applications, a member is normally expected to serve on one or more of the numerous statutory and voluntary bodies operating in the area of the local authority. Some members of the council may, for example, be invited to serve on the area health authority, the community health council, the regional water authority, the local valuation court or the governing body of a school or technical college. Others may be invited to serve on the citizens' advice bureau, the local council of social service, the marriage guidance council, the accident prevention council or the local chamber of commerce. Further demands may be made on a member's time by political party meetings. He may, for example, be expected to attend meetings of his ward committee, which are held at regular intervals, party meetings at district level and the Annual General Meeting of his local association and of his ward.

Functions

The activities of a council member may also include attendance at functions. The Mayor, for example, may hold an annual charity ball in aid of local charities to which all councillors with their wives or husbands are invited; and there may be other mayoral functions—e.g. the annual civic reception. A member, especially if he is a governor or manager of schools, will be invited to school prizegivings. The political party to which the member belongs may hold dinner dances, garden parties, theatre parties, summer fairs, Christmas fêtes, motor car rallies, etc., with social or political objects in mind and for the purpose of raising party funds. Active party members, including councillors, are expected not only to attend these functions but also to help with their organisation.

Constituency inquiries and complaints

Some of the most valuable and important work undertaken by a member relates to inquiries and complaints from constituents. A councillor may receive letters from constituents addressed to his home or to the town hall; he may receive telephone calls from constituents, and occasionally they may call on him at his private address. Sometimes a constituent may take the opportunity of airing a personal grievance in the course of a chance meeting with his councillor at a function. Many complaints relating to local government are referred to councillors by MPs, who feel that, although the constituent contacted his MP in the first instance, the matter is one related to the work of the council and could, therefore, be dealt with more appropriately and expeditiously by a councillor. Inquiries and complaints cover a very wide range of the council's activities, particularly in relation to education, housing and planning. Sometimes the complaint is frivolous or trivial, or comes from a crank; nevertheless the councillor will investigate it for fear of losing local political support.

Many of the complaints concerning education relate to choice of school. In most areas there are schools which are heavily oversubscribed, whilst others find it difficult to attract pupils. Parents who have chosen what they consider to be the most desirable or the most conveniently situated school in the area are naturally dissatisfied if their children are placed in a different school, and some parents seek redress by contacting their councillor. In exceptional circumstances the councillor, after eliciting the full facts and contacting the chief education officer, may succeed in his efforts to satisfy the parents, but it is obvious that if a school is very popular some of the parents who choose it must be disappointed.

A large number of the inquiries and complaints pertain-

Pressure on councillors' time

The work of a councillor is often very time-consuming, and some councillors who have demanding full-time jobs find themselves under heavy pressure. This is particularly so when the councillor is leader of the council (i.e. in effect, the local Prime Minister) or chairman of a main committee— e.g. the education committee or the housing committee. When the dominant party on the council wishes to explain important new legislation or proposals, or to give them the widest publicity, the chairman of the appropriate committee may find that he is faced with considerable work. If, for example, an authority which has a selective system of secondary education wishes to change to a non-selective— i.e. a comprehensive—system, the chairman of the education committee may find it necessary to hold a series of public meetings in a number of school halls throughout the area of the authority to which the parents are invited. These meetings may also be attended by the leader of the council, the vice-chairman of the education committee and the shadow chairman of the education committee, representing the opposition. A similar position could arise in relation to housing. Thus, public meetings of this kind were arranged in some areas to explain, publicise and debate the rent increases foreshadowed by the Housing Finance Act, 1972. Many public-spirited employers give full recognition to the fact that councillors in their employ are devoting the greater part of their leisure time in the public interest and, as far as possible, allow them time off from their work. The Confederation of British Industry and other bodies of employers have circularised their members drawing attention to the importance the Government attaches to local authority membership, and asking them to adopt a generous attitude to employees wishing to undertake public duties and to give sympathetic consideration to requests for release. The Government itself has set a good example by allowing civil servants who are councillors a maximum of eighteen days' special leave a year.

The work load of a councillor, and even more so of a councillor who is leader of the council or of the opposition, or chairman of a main committee, could be considerably reduced if secretarial help were provided by the council. The Bains Committee (1972) recommended that in all authorities provision should be made for basic secretarial services to be available to members. Since the publication of this report a number of local authorities have provided support services for councillors—e.g. a typing and photo-copying service for correspondence received from con-stituents.

Payment of members

Until the reorganisation of local government on 1 April 1974, councillors were virtually unpaid. Although local authorities, with the exception of parish councils and parish meetings, were empowered to pay their mayor or chairman an allowance, other members of local authorities—unlike MPs, who are paid a salary—were entitled only to travelling and subsistence allowances and to 'financial loss allowances'. Under the Local Government Act, 1948, and the Public Authorities (Allowances) Act, 1961, members of local authorities and co-opted members of committees and sub-committees were entitled to reasonable travelling expenses and subsistence allowances and to financial loss allowances for approved duty—e.g. for attendance at council, com-mittee or subcommittee meetings, or at an inspection.

Financial loss allowances were intended to cover loss of earnings or expenses necessarily incurred by a member in performing an approved duty. They were justified by the Lindsay Committee on the Expenses of Members of Local Authorities (1947) on the ground that 'local authorities should be able to draw their members from the widest pos-sible section of the public, and should not be deprived of the service of any man or woman who is fitted to serve by ability or experience'. The Committee were of the opinion that 'if

Highway lighting
Traffic and parking
Transport planning
Refuse disposal
Parks and open spaces (concurrent powers with district councils)
Consumer protection (i.e. weights and measures, trade description, food and drugs, etc.)
Police (subject to amalgamation schemes)
Fire (subject to amalgamation schemes)
Museums and art galleries (concurrent powers with district councils)
Town development (concurrent powers with district councils)
Smallholdings
Airports (concurrent powers with district councils)

All districts
Housing, including provision, management, slum clearance and improvements
Planning, including the preparation of local plans and development control
Maintenance of footpaths
Off-street parking (in accordance with the county transportation plan)
Environmental health, including clean air, infectious diseases and slaughter houses
Refuse collection
Building regulations
Cemeteries and crematoria
Parks and open spaces (concurrent powers with county council)
Airports (concurrent powers with county council)
Museums and art galleries (concurrent powers with county council)
Town development (concurrent powers with county council)

Making and levying of rates
Licensing of theatres and cinemas
Registration of local land charges

In Wales the position is similar to that of England (outside London), except that district councils are responsible not only for refuse collection but also for disposal, and they may also exceptionally be entrusted with libraries, weights and measures, and food and drugs functions.

Parishes and communities have only minor functions, which relate to such matters as village greens, footpaths, the provision of seats and shelters, public clocks, and parking places for motor cycles and bicycles. As regards allotments, the position in England is that parish councils and meetings are allotment authorities, but where there is no parish council or meeting the function is exercised by the district council. In Wales allotments are the concurrent responsibility of district and community councils. Before the coming into operation of the Local Government Act, 1972, parish councils had only limited powers of rate expenditure, but these limitations no longer apply to parishes, and they have not been applied to communities.

A more detailed exposition of local government functions will be given in the respective chapters devoted to individual services or groups of services provided by local authorities. The distribution of functions in London will be dealt with in Chapter 20.

It will be seen from the information given above that the functions of non-metropolitan county councils are wider than those of metropolitan county councils, and that the functions of metropolitan districts are more extensive than those of non-metropolitan districts. The differences relate to education, libraries and the personal social services. In metropolitan counties these services are the responsibility of the district councils, whilst in non-metropolitan counties it is the county council which administers them. The functions of the council of a district which has become a borough are no different from those of a district council. As county borough councils have ceased to exist there are now no all-purpose authorities – i.e. authorities which are responsible for all the local government functions in the area. The metropolitan district councils are the nearest approach to all-purpose authorities but even they do not administer the services listed above under 'all counties', which are deemed to require a more extensive area than the district for their more efficient administration. In London the local authority approximately comparable to the metropolitan district is the outer London borough.

The services provided by local authorities even of the same status vary from one area to another for the following reasons:

1 Some of the services provided by local authorities are obligatory whilst others are optional. A metropolitan district, for example, as local education authority, *must* provide sufficient schools in its area, but the same council, as housing authority, *may* sell council houses to council tenants.

2 Some local authorities have obtained additional powers by local Acts to administer services which they are not allowed to provide by the general law. Thus, Birmingham City Council obtained powers by a local Act in 1919 to establish a municipal bank.

3 The power to delegate functions is used more extensively by some authorities than by others. Thus, some highway functions may be delegated by a county council to a district council, and agency arrangements may be made by a county council with a district council in relation not only to highway powers but also to such functions as town and country planning, refuse disposal and consumer protection. When limited use is made of such powers, the services administered by the county council are more extensive and the services administered by the district council correspondingly less extensive, and *vice versa*.

4 Local authorities sometimes combine to form joint authorities for special functions—e.g. joint library boards and joint planning authorities.

It is clear, therefore, that the services provided by local authorities, even within the same category, may differ considerably from one area to another.

Types of services provided

Apart from the division of services into those which are obligatory and those which are optional, the services provided by local authorities may be classified in several ways. There are, for instance, environmental and personal services, and trading and non-trading services. Environmental services are those which are provided for a locality, as distinct from personal services, which are rendered to the inhabitants of a locality as individuals. Environmental services include the collection and disposal of refuse, the control of buildings, street lighting and the maintenance of highways. Included in personal services are education, the care of children deprived of a normal home life, the provision of school meals and the care of the aged. Trading services are services such as the maintenance of municipal bus services, the control of markets and the maintenance of civic restaurants—services which the local authority hopes will be run at a profit, or at any rate, will be self-supporting. Non-trading services are those services which are a charge on public funds.

The doctrine of *ultra vires*

The activities of local authorities are confined to those which may be undertaken in pursuance of a statute. Local authorities have no general power to exercise functions merely because they are not prohibited by statute: the scope of their work is limited to those functions which they are expressly empowered to exercise by Act of Parliament or are functions which are incidental to the powers expressly conferred upon them. This limitation of the powers of local authorities is known as the doctrine of *ultra vires*.

Before the coming into operation of the Local Government Act, 1972, municipal corporations—i.e. county borough councils and borough councils outside London—having been incorporated by Royal Charter, were distinguished from other local authorities, which were statutory corporations. They were in theory exempt from the doctrine of *ultra vires*, but in practice the restrictions imposed on their freedom of action did not differ materially from those applying. to other local authorities. Municipal corporations, however, having common law powers in addition to their statutory powers, were not so rigorously limited in their activities as were statutory corporations. But now that all local authorities (except the City of London Corporation) are, under the Act of 1972, statutory corporations, there are no exemptions from *ultra vires*. Even those district councils which have acquired the dignity of borough status are all. legally in the same position as other local authorities.

The Maud Committee on the Management of Local Government, which issued its main report in 1967, recommended that, subject to appropriate safeguards, the *ultra vires* rule should be abolished; and the Royal Commission on Local Government (1969) proposed that all main authorities should have a general power to spend money for the benefit of their areas and inhabitants. The Local Government Act, 1972, whilst not accepting these proposals, adopted a practical compromise. The position now is that an authority may incur expenditure which is 'in the interests of their area or any part of it or all or some of its inhabitants', provided that a rating limit of 2p in the £ is not exceeded in any financial year. This provision enables local authorities, albeit within strict financial limits, to widen the scope of their activities despite the continued existence of the *ultra vires* rule.

T–D

The transfer of services from small to larger authorities

There has been a significant trend, particularly since the end of the Second World War, in favour of transferring services to the larger local government units. Many services which were originally parochial functions are now the responsibility of the second-tier authorities—i.e. district councils—or the county council, and some services which were formerly administered by small second-tier authorities—i.e. borough, urban and rural district councils—are now administered by the new and larger district councils or by county councils. The following are examples of this tendency:

1 *Poor relief*
Under the Poor Law Act, 1601, the local government area for the relief of the poor was the parish. The Poor Law Amendment Act, 1834, substituted the union (a combination of parishes) for the parish, and the Local Government Act, 1929, substituted the county and the county borough for the union. Under the National Assistance Act, 1948, the Poor Law was abolished, and financial assistance to persons in need is, in general, no longer the responsibility of local authorities,[1] but the provision of residential accommodation for the aged and other persons in need of care and attention was cast upon the county and the county borough. The Local Government Act, 1972, has now transferred these powers to the non-metropolitan county councils and the metropolitan district councils. In London these powers are exercised by the London boroughs and the City of London Corporation.

2 *Education*
Under the Elementary Education Act, 1870, a school board was set up for each school district, and the school district

[1] Now the responsibility of the Department of Health and Social Security.

was the parish or the borough. The Education Act, 1902, substituted the area of the local education authority[1] for the smaller school board area, and the Education Act, 1944, transferred responsibility for education to the county or county borough. The new local education authorities under the Local Government Act, 1972, are the councils of non-metropolitan counties and metropolitan districts. In London the education authorities are the Inner London Education Authority and the twenty outer London boroughs.

3 Police

Until 1835 law and order outside London was mainly a parish responsibility. The Municipal Corporations Act, 1835, substituted the borough for the parish in the chartered towns, and the County Police Act, 1839, substituted the county for the parish outside the boroughs. Under the Police Act, 1946, the unit for police purposes was normally the county or county borough, but the Police Act, 1964, created larger units. Under the Local Government Act, 1972, the new police authorities outside the Metropolitan Police District are the county authorities or combined police authorities, covering the area of two or more counties.

4 Highways

Under the Highways Act, 1555, the local government area for the maintenance of highways was the parish. The Local Government Act, 1888, made the county responsible for the maintenance of main roads in rural areas, and under the Highways Act, 1959, the county became the authority for the maintenance of all roads, except trunk roads, and unclassified roads in urban areas.[2] Under the Local Government Act, 1972, the county council is the highway

---

[1] The local education authorities under the Education Act, 1902, were the county councils, the county borough councils and (for elementary education only) the larger borough and urban district councils.

[2] Subject to a claim by the county district to have powers delegated.

authority, but district councils may claim maintenance powers for some urban roads.

The transfer of services from the smaller to the larger local authorities can be justified on several grounds. During the past three-quarters of a century the marked improvement in transport and communications has facilitated the organisation of public services covering larger areas. During the same period local authorities have been entrusted with services, such as town and country planning, which require large areas for their administration. Mergers in the world of industry and commerce are not without their influence on the structure of local government. The transfer of services to the larger local authorities is also justified on the grounds that the financial burden can thereby be spread more evenly and that the operation of services over larger areas is conducive to administrative efficiency. There is, of course, the contrary view that local government should be as local as possible, and that bigger is not necessarily better. There is the fear that larger areas of administration could lead to local government being conducted in an atmosphere of remote control and soulless bureaucracy. It is unquestionably true to say that the transfer of functions to larger local authorities has not resulted in significant reductions in public expenditure, and the contention that changes of this character have been justified on grounds of improved efficiency is debatable.

The transfer of services from local authorities to the state

Side by side with the process of transferring functions to the major local authorities at the expense of the smaller authorities, there has been a strong tendency, especially during the past three or four decades, to transfer services from local authorities to the state or to public corporations. (This movement has already been referred to in Chapter 2.)

Thus, by the Unemployment Act, 1934, the responsibility for the able-bodied unemployed was transferred from the county councils and the county borough councils to the Unemployment Assistance Board. By the Trunk Roads Acts, 1936 and 1946, the responsibility for the maintenance of trunk roads—i.e. roads for the main arteries of traffic— was transferred from local authorities to the Minister of Transport.[1] By the National Health Service Act, 1946, local authority hospitals were transferred to the Minister of Health. By the Electricity Act, 1947, electricity supply was transferred from local authorities to the British Electricity Authority; and by the Gas Act, 1948, gas supply was transferred from local authorities to Area Gas Boards. By the Local Government Act, 1948, the valuation of property for rating was transferred from local authorities to the Board of Inland Revenue. The Housing Finance Act, 1972, virtually removed from local authorities and transferred to the Department of the Environment the power to fix the rents of council houses. By the Water Act, 1973, responsibility for water supply, river pollution, sewerage and sewage disposal was transferred to nine regional water authorities. And by the National Health Service Reorganisation Act, 1973, the personal health services for which local authorities were responsible were entrusted to area health Authorities.

This is indeed a very impressive catalogue of transfers of local government powers to central government or to regional authorities outside the sphere of local government, but local authorities have obtained partial compensation for the loss of these services by the acquisition of important new functions. For example, the planning powers and duties of local authorities were augmented by the Town and Country Planning Act, 1947, and by subsequent legislation; and their functions relating to the care of children were increased by the Children Act, 1948, and by the Children and Young Persons Act, 1963. In 1948 local authorities also

[1] These Acts provided that the Minister could delegate his function of maintenance to local authorities.

acquired new powers with regard to entertainments, and power to provide accommodation for the aged and infirm (Local Government Act, 1948, and National Assistance Act, 1948, respectively). More recently, they have been entrusted with new or additional functions, such as those conferred by the Civic Amenities Act, 1967, the National Health Service (Family Planning) Act, 1967, the Trade Descriptions Act, 1968, the Local Authority Social Services Act, 1970, and the Land Compensation Act, 1973.

8 Education

At the beginning of the nineteenth century education was not regarded by all sections of the community as the concern of the state. The policy of *laissez-faire*, to which the Government was committed, required that there should be the minimum interference with private enterprise and, in particular, that the long hours and the deplorable conditions under which adults and children worked in mines, mills, factories and workshops should remain unregulated. Any proposal to provide instruction for the children of the masses out of the public purse, quite apart from opposition it aroused for reasons of expense, was regarded with suspicion and misgiving by many of the manufacturers and landowners in the unreformed House of Commons, as it threatened to deprive them of a cheap source of labour. Bills for the establishment of parochial schools were introduced by Samuel Whitbread (1807) and Brougham (1820), and in 1833 John Arthur Roebuck brought in an ambitious Bill proposing universal education. Further Bills were introduced in 1853 and 1855, but they failed to reach the statute book, largely owing to disagreement among the religious bodies associated with the cause of popular education.

At the time when these proposals were being made to provide education for the children of the lower classes there were four types of school which poor children could attend. There were the 'charity schools', established under the auspices of the Society for Promoting Christian Knowledge, which was founded in 1699. In these schools no fees were paid, as their expenses were defrayed by endowments and voluntary contributions. This type of school was declining in importance by the beginning of the nineteenth century. There were also the 'dame schools' or private adventure schools, frequently conducted by persons with no qualifications or aptitude for the work. The end of the eighteenth century saw the establishment of Sunday schools on a large scale, but the most extensive efforts to provide popular education were made by two religious societies—namely, the National Society, which was closely identified with the Church of England, and the British and Foreign School Society, which was set up by the Nonconformists. The voluntary schools established by these two societies were maintained by voluntary subscriptions and school fees. Their aim was to provide education for large numbers of children as cheaply as possible, and, in order to achieve this object, they made use of the monitorial system, under which the older children taught the younger children and the role of the teacher was confined to general supervision of the monitors and the punishment of pupils. The technique of instruction given in this way was necessarily mechanical, and it was frequently found that the children scarcely understood the meaning of passages which they had learnt to read.

Whilst these efforts were being made to widen the scope of popular education, a sum of £20 000 was voted by Treasury Minute in 1833 for the erection of school buildings. It was to be paid to the schools maintained by the National Society and the British and Foreign School Society, and no grant was to be made unless at least half the cost was met by voluntary contributions. The annual vote was increased in 1839 to £30 000, and in the same year a special Committee of the Privy Council was established to administer the grant, and inspectors of schools were appointed. By 1852 the Government grant in aid of education had increased to

£160 000, but it was not until 1870 that education became a local government function.

The Elementary Education Act, 1870

This Act divided the country into school districts, consisting of boroughs and parishes. In those school districts where educational facilities were inadequate, school boards were to be elected: in boroughs by the burgesses—i.e. the borough electors—and elsewhere by the ratepayers. London was to be a separate school district. The school boards were empowered to establish and maintain public elementary schools. Fees not exceeding 9*d.* a week could be charged, and where the revenue from Government grants and school fees proved insufficient the school boards could meet the deficiency from the rates. In the board schools religious instruction was to be of a non-denominational character, and parents were to be given the right to withdraw their children from religious instruction. The voluntary schools, which continued to function, were to be allowed to give religious instruction of a denominational character, subject to the right of withdrawal mentioned above. These voluntary schools were not entitled to receive any rate aid, but continued to qualify for Government grants.

The Act of 1870 was essentially a compromise. By establishing school boards and retaining the voluntary schools, it set up the dual system, which, with modifications, is still in existence today. Henceforth there were to be two types of elementary school: the board schools, maintained by rates, Government grants and fees; and the voluntary schools, maintained by fees and subscriptions, with the assistance of Government grants, but receiving no aid from the rates. The Act did not provide for universal compulsory attendance, but this object was achieved by later Acts (in 1876 and 1880).

Towards the close of the century the London School Board and many school boards in the North of England with progressive ideas on their responsibilities as education authorities established 'higher grade' schools, where the instruction given included science and art.[1] Some of the voluntary schools would gladly have followed their example, but as the teaching of these subjects entailed the provision of expensive accommodation and equipment they found themselves unable to compete with the board schools, which derived part of their revenue from rates. As the scope of education widened and it became more costly to administer, the financial position of the voluntary schools became more critical, and they found themselves in a position of inferiority compared with the board schools. The need to put the voluntary schools on an equal footing with the board schools and to extend the system of public education to include higher education became manifest, and this purpose was achieved by the Education Act, 1902.

The Education Act, 1902

This Act abolished schools boards,[2] transferring their functions to county councils, to county borough councils and also to the larger borough and urban district councils, who were to be the authorities for elementary education only. The new local education authority was made responsible for secular education in voluntary schools, and the county councils and county borough councils were required to consider the educational needs of their areas and to supply or aid the supply of higher education. In accordance with this provision, local education authorities established a considerable number of new secondary schools (now termed grammar schools), and a number of existing secondary schools were assisted or taken over.

---

[1] This policy of the London School Board was challenged by the District Auditor (the Cockerton Judgment, 1900).

[2] It also abolished school attendance committees, which had been set up in 1876 in areas where there was no school board.

The Education Act, 1918

The scope of public education was further widened by the Education Act, 1918 (the Fisher Act), which finally abolished fees in elementary schools, raised the minimum school-leaving age to the end of the school term in which the pupil attained the age of 14, and empowered local education authorities to establish nursery schools for children between 2 and 5 years of age. The Act also required local education authorities to establish day continuation schools, in which boys and girls between the ages of 14 and 18 could receive compulsory part-time instruction; but as the operation of this part of the Act was postponed, pupils attending day continuation schools did so voluntarily. The law relating to education was consolidated in the Education Act, 1921.

The Education Act, 1944

During the Second World War widespread interest was shown in education, and although divergent views were held on the form which the reorganisation of the educational system should take it was generally agreed that full educational opportunities should be afforded to all who could take advantage of them. The Education Act, 1944, repealed the earlier legislation and restated the new system of national education. Alterations in the law have been made in a number of subsequent Acts, the last of which was the Local Government Act, 1972. The following were the most important features of the 1944 Act which effected changes in the law:

1 The creation of a new central authority (the Ministry of Education in place of the Board of Education).
2 The substitution of county councils and county borough councils for the local education authorities in existence before the operation of the Act, and the creation of divisional executives and 'excepted districts'.
3 The organisation of the educational system in three

progressive stages (to be known as primary, secondary
and further education) in place of the former division
into elementary and higher education.

4 The abolition of fees in all maintained secondary
schools.

5 The raising of the minimum school-leaving age to the
end of the term in which the pupil attained the age of
15 (with provision for the raising of the age to 16 at a
later date by Order in Council).

6 Wider provision of nursery schools and nursery classes.

7 Wider provision for the welfare of children and for
handicapped children.

8 The registration and inspection of independent schools.

These changes receive further consideration below.

The central authority

The Board of Education, which was established in 1899 as
the central authority for education in England and Wales,
was replaced by the Ministry of Education; the political
head of the Department was the Minister of Education, who
could be a member of the Cabinet. Under the Education
Act, 1944, the Minister was required 'to promote the education of the people of England and Wales and the progressive development of institutions devoted to that purpose
and to secure the effective execution by local authorities,
under his control and direction, of the national policy for
providing a varied and comprehensive educational service
in every area'. In carrying out his duties the Minister was
advised by two Central Advisory Councils, one for England
and one for Wales. In 1964 the functions of the Minister of
Education were transferred to the Secretary of State for
Education and Science, and later in that year the Secretary
of State for Wales was entrusted with responsibility for
primary and secondary education in Wales.

The local education authorities under the Education Act, 1944

Under the Education Act, 1944, the local education authorities for all forms of education were normally the county councils and the county borough councils. Each local education authority was required to establish an education committee. The majority of its members were required to be members of the local education authority, and the committee had to include people of experience in education and people acquainted with educational conditions in the area. To fulfil this requirement many local education authorities included teachers in the employ of the authority as co-opted members of the education committee and its subcommittees. The local education authority was empowered to delegate all or any of its functions to the education committee, with the exception of levying a rate or borrowing money.

In order to obtain the full benefit of local knowledge and experience and, as far as possible, to decentralise the administration of education, some counties were, in accordance with a scheme approved by the Department of Education and Science, split up into divisions. In each of these divisions there was a body known as a divisional executive, to which some of the educational functions of the county council were delegated. These divisional executives consisted of representatives of the non-county borough or district council and the local education authority, and also of co-opted members. A large non-country borough or urban district, however, could be excepted from the general scheme of delegation and its council entrusted with the functions of a divisional executive, in which case the borough or urban district was known as an 'excepted district'. These excepted districts were, in fact, a special type of divisional executive. The functions delegated to divisional executives and excepted districts varied considerably from one area to another, but the levying of a rate or the raising of a loan could not be delegated. There were no divisional executives or excepted districts in the area of the Inner London Education Authority.

The local education authorities under the Local Government Act, 1972

The new local education authorities under the Local Government Act, 1972, are the councils of non-metropolitan counties and metropolitan districts. In London since 1965 educational provision for the area of the twelve inner London boroughs and the City of London has been the responsibility of the Inner London Education Authority, and the twenty outer London boroughs have been the local education authorities. The local education authorities in England are now, therefore, as follows:

Non-metropolitan county councils	39
Metropolitan district councils	36
London borough councils	20
Inner London Education Authority	1
Total	96

In Wales the local education authorities are the eight county councils. There are now no divisional executives or excepted districts, but the requirements in the Education Act, 1944, for the establishment of an education committee and the arrangements for the inclusion of co-opted members remain unchanged. There has been no change in the central authority, and the Secretary of State for Education and Science has always had a seat in the Cabinet.

Primary, secondary and further education

The Education Act, 1944, requires that, so far as is compatible with efficient instruction and training and the avoidance of unreasonable public expenditure, pupils should be educated in accordance with the wishes of their parents, and that all pupils should be afforded opportunities for education suited to their ages, abilities and aptitudes. This does not mean, however, that a parent has an unfettered choice of school for his child. Some parents have ambitious aspirations for their children which bear little or no relation to their ability, and these ambitions are sometimes reflected in the choice of school. Although local education authorities endeavour, as far as possible, to meet the wishes of parents, it would be administratively impossible to satisfy the wishes of all parents, especially in areas where there are schools which are very popular and highly oversubscribed. Provision for the education of children is not necessarily confined to instruction at school. In approved cases arrangements for teaching in the children's homes are made—e.g. for crippled children who are unable to walk or for children suffering from school phobia.

The Education Act, 1944, abolished the former distinction between elementary and higher education, and the three stages of primary, secondary and further education were substituted. Normally the primary stage is full-time education from the age of 5 to 11, and the secondary stage from 11 upwards. Further education is full or part-time education for persons over the compulsory school age who are not continuing full-time education at a secondary school.

Until the early 1950s there were three main types of secondary education: grammar, technical and modern— throughout the whole country. The grammar school still provides an academic education up to the age of at least 16 (for many pupils up to the age of 18 or 19), leading mainly to the universities and the professions. The secondary technical school, at which the average leaving age is lower than at the grammar school, provides courses of instruction related to industry or commerce and meets the requirements of pupils with an aptitude for practical work. The aim of the secondary modern school is to provide a good general education for pupils until the age of 16 (and for some pupils beyond that age) suited to their intellectual abilities. Some local education authorities have, since the end of the Second World War, established what are known as comprehensive schools, to provide all three forms of secondary education—grammar, technical and modern—in one large school, though not necessarily under one roof; and in 1965 the Secretary of State for Education and Science announced the adoption of a national policy involving the reorganisation of secondary education on comprehensive lines. Until the advent of comprehensive schools, about 20% of the children who left the primary schools were transferred to grammar schools and a comparatively small number to secondary technical schools, the remainder receiving their education after the age of 11 in secondary modern schools. These arrangements are still in operation in those areas where comprehensive education has not yet been introduced. (In 1972 41% of secondary school pupils aged 13 attended comprehensive schools, 36% attended secondary modern schools, 13% went to grammar schools and the remainder went to other schools, including technical schools). The method of allocating pupils to the three types of secondary schools, which are outside the comprehensive system, differs considerably from one area to another, but most local education authorities base their selection at least partly on the result of an '11-plus examination', which is held annually, or on a series of informal tests extending over a long period. The great majority of local education authorities have by now introduced reorganisation schemes on comprehensive lines covering the whole or part of their area, or have had their schemes approved by the Secretary of State. Some local education authorities have established sixth-form colleges to which all pupils who stay at school after reaching the age of 16 are transferred. These sixth-form colleges cater for all ranges of ability, providing both academic courses and courses of a practical nature.

About two-thirds of the primary and secondary schools

maintained by local education authorities are county schools—i.e. they were established by the local education authorities or their predecessors—and the remaining third, which were built by voluntary bodies (mainly religious bodies, e.g. the Church of England and the Roman Catholic Church), are voluntary schools.[1] The local education authority is represented on the governing bodies of these voluntary schools, but the managers or governors[2] are allowed considerable autonomy in the conduct of their schools, particularly with regard to the appointment and dismissal of teachers and to religious instruction. The relationship between the managers or governors of a voluntary school and the local education authority are set out in the rules of management of a primary school and in the articles of government of a secondary school. The rules of management of a primary school and the articles of a county secondary school are made by the local education authority (the articles with the approval of the Secretary of State for Education and Science). The articles of government of a voluntary secondary school are made by the Secretary of State after consultation with the local education authority.

Local education authorities, in addition to their responsibilities for primary and secondary education, are required under the Act to make provision for their area of adequate facilities for further education—i.e. full-time and part-time education for persons over compulsory school age who are

[1] There are three classes of voluntary schools—voluntary aided, voluntary controlled and special agreement schools—and the powers and duties of the managers or governors on the one hand and the local education authorities on the other are largely dependent upon the class to which the voluntary school belongs.

[2] School managers and governors are appointed by both county and voluntary schools—managers for primary schools and governors for secondary schools. The powers of the managers and governors of county schools are not as wide as those of voluntary schools. In recent years some schools have included on their governing and managing bodies parents of pupils attending the school and elected representatives of the teaching and non-teaching staff, and some secondary schools have included pupils as governors.

not continuing full-time education at a secondary school. The field of further education (including higher education) is a very extensive one, covering full-time and part-time vocational education in polytechnics, technical and commercial colleges and other establishments, the youth service and recreational activities, mainly in evening institutes. Large numbers of young people in technical colleges etc. are released by their employers for one day a week or on block release—e.g. full-time for six or eight weeks in the year—for vocational studies. The wide range of leisure-time occupations in which instruction is available in some areas even includes classes in subjects such as fishing, boxing, ballroom dancing, wrestling, archery, bee-keeping, fencing and Esperanto.

The abolition of fees in maintained secondary schools

Since 1 April 1945, no fees have been charged at schools maintained by local education authorities—i.e. at county or voluntary schools—except to pupils who are provided with board and lodging. Before that date, fees were payable by some of the pupils attending secondary schools. Fees may still be charged for further education. Fees may also be paid by pupils attending direct-grant schools—i.e. schools which receive a direct grant from the Department of Education and Science—and, of course, by pupils attending independent schools.

The raising of the school-leaving age

The Education Act, 1918, raised the minimum school-leaving age to the end of the school term in which the pupil attained the age of 14 and the Education Act, 1944, substituted the age of 15 for 14 with effect from 1947. The Act made provision for the raising of the minimum school-leaving age to 16 by Order in Council as soon as the

Secretary of State was satisfied that sufficient buildings and teachers were available, and an Order was made bringing this change into operation in 1972. A child cannot necessarily leave school immediately after reaching his sixteenth birthday. If, for example, he attains the age of 16 in September, he must remain at school until the following Easter, and if he reaches the age of 16 in February, he cannot leave school until the following July.

Nursery schools and nursery classes

Before the operation of the Education Act, 1944, local education authorities had power to provide nursery schools for children between 2 and 5 years of age, and some nursery schools were provided by voluntary bodies. It is now the duty of the local education authority to provide nursery schools and nursery classes, but the shortage of teachers and accommodation as well as financial considerations have impeded the establishment of new nursery schools and classes, with the result that in most areas the demand for places in nursery schools and nursery classes at present greatly exceeds the number of places available.[1] In 1972 the Conservative Government announced in a White Paper an ambitious programme for the expansion of nursery education. Within the next ten years nursery education was to be made available without charge to those children aged 3 and 4 whose parents wished to benefit from it. Nursery education was generally to be on a half-time basis—i.e. some of the children attending in the morning and the others in the afternoon—but on educational and social grounds about 15% of the children were to be allowed to attend full-time. The scheme has not yet been put into operation.

[1] No fees are payable in nursery schools or nursery classes provided by local education authorities, but fees related to the means of the parents are charged for young children up to the age of 5 who attend day nurseries, which are the responsibility of the social services department of the local authority and have a social rather than an educational purpose.

The welfare of children and handicapped children

It has long been recognised that a child may not be able to derive the maximum benefit from the education he receives unless full attention is given to his general welfare. Even before the operation of the Education Act, 1944, local education authorities were required to provide medical treatment in elementary schools and were empowered to provide such treatment in secondary schools. They were also empowered to provide meals and milk for children attending elementary schools. The Act of 1944 imposed a duty on the local education authority to provide medical inspection and treatment at all schools maintained by them—i.e. at all county and voluntary schools—but under the National Health Service Reorganisation Act, 1973, this function was transferred on 1 April 1974 to the area health authority.

Local education authorities are required by the Education Act, 1944, to provide midday dinners at all maintained schools, and they must now provide free milk for children up to the age of 7. Normally a charge is made for each dinner, subject to remission in approved cases, but milk is provided free of charge. About two-thirds of the children in maintained schools are provided with school dinners, and an even higher percentage of the children in infant schools are provided with school milk.

Boarding education may be provided for children for whom education as boarders is considered desirable by their parents and the local education authority. The authority may also provide clothing for a pupil to enable him to attend school if he cannot take full advantage of the education which he is receiving owing to inadequate clothing.

The Children and Young Persons Act, 1933, imposes restrictions on the employment of children attending school, and a child under 13 years of age may not be employed at all, unless he obtains a licence issued by the local education authority. Local education authorities may prohibit certain types of employment—e.g. lathering in a barber's shop or helping in a billiard saloon—and some authorities have prohibited any employment until the child reaches the age of 14. Local education authorities may make it a condition that the child shall be medically examined before an employment permit is granted, and the Education Act, 1944, empowers an authority to prohibit or limit any employment which is prejudicial to a child's health or otherwise renders him unfit to take full advantage of his education.

Under the Children and Young Persons Acts, 1933 and 1963, a person under the age of 17 may not take part in street trading, except when he is employed by his parents, and bylaws may be made by the local education authority regulating or prohibiting street trading by persons under the age of 18.

Under the 1944 Act the local education authority is required to arrange for the provision of free transport to and from the school which the pupil attends, unless the school attended is within walking distance from home. Where free transport is not provided, reasonable travelling expenses may be paid by the local education authority.

The Act also deals with handicapped children. Previous enactments provided for the compulsory attendance of blind and deaf children at special schools from the age of 5 to 16 years and for mentally defective children from 7 to 16 years. The 1944 Act requires the local education authority to provide education for the less severely handicapped children in the ordinary primary and secondary schools, and for the severely handicapped children in special schools. The number of categories of handicapped children was increased, and all handicapped children at special schools are required to attend from the age of 5 to 16.

The registration and inspection of independent schools

An independent school is a school which receives no grant from the Department of Education and Science or from a local education authority. Some local education authorities do, however, pay the fees of a limited number of pupils resident in their area who attend independent schools. These schools are widely diverse in character: they range from small private schools conducted for profit to the large public boarding schools, many of which are very old foundations. Independent schools are dealt with in Part III of the Education Act, 1944, which was brought into operation in 1957. The Act provides for a register to be kept at the Department of all independent schools, and for these schools to be open to inspection by the Department's inspectors.

Education finance

Education is by far the most costly of all the services provided by local authorities, and it accounts for about 40% of the total expenditure incurred by local authorities. In 1945 the nation spent only about 1·7% of the gross national product on education, but about 6·5% of the gross national product—i.e. about £3500 million—was spent on education in 1973–4. The number of pupils at school in England and Wales exceeds nine million, and more than one person in four is now a student at a school, college, polytechnic or university. Although local education authorities are not the sole providers of education, they bear the brunt of the responsibility and initially by far the greater part of the cost.

A block grant, known as the rate support grant, is paid by the Exchequer to local authorities in respect of most of their services, including education. This grant is distributed to local authorities in accordance with a formula which is designed to ensure that the most needy authorities derive the greatest benefit. About two-thirds of the cost of education is in this way defrayed by the Exchequer, and Government aid for mandatory awards to students—i.e. for degree and comparable courses—and for teacher training is given at the rate of 90%.

Public libraries as an adjunct to the educational system

The importance of public libraries in any educational system needs no emphasis. It was not until 1850 that local authorities were empowered to provide public libraries. The Public Libraries Act of that year enabled borough councils with a population of not less than 10 000 to provide libraries, subject to a rating limit of $\frac{1}{2}d.$ in the £. These authorities were not allowed to spend money on the purchase of books—apparently it was assumed that gifts of books from private donors would meet all requirements. The Act was not passed without serious misgiving on the part of some members of the House of Commons, who feared that public libraries would become 'schools of agitation'.

The limit of a rate of $\frac{1}{2}d.$ in the £ was increased to $1d.$ in 1855, and under the Public Libraries Act, 1892, every borough, urban district and rural parish was to be a library district, and parishes were allowed to combine for library purposes. Library authorities were empowered to establish public libraries, museums and art galleries. Libraries provided by local authorities were assisted by grants made by Andrew Carnegie, who made large donations for buildings and equipment.

The Public Libraries Act, 1919, abolished the rating limit of $1d.$ in the £ and authorised county councils to become library authorities for those parts of the county in which the Public Libraries Acts were not already in operation. The Public Libraries and Museums Act, 1964, incorporated many of the recommendations of the Roberts Committee on the Public Library Service, which had reported in 1959. The Library authorities under that Act were the county and county borough councils and, generally speaking, the councils of non-county boroughs and urban districts with a population of 40 000 or more. Under the Local Government Act, 1972, the library authorities in

England are now the councils of non-metropolitan counties and metropolitan districts (in London, the London borough councils and the City of London Corporation). In Wales the library authorities are the county councils, but district councils may exceptionally be made responsible for this function. In recent years some library authorities have expanded the scope of their activities by lending gramophone records, tapes and prints as well as books. Many local libraries are part of larger systems, and books may often be speedily obtained from another branch of the same library. Some libraries now offer an inquiry answering service, which provides information on an infinite variety of subjects. Most schools now have a school lending library and some have a reference library, which the pupils are encouraged to use as much as possible.

9　The Social Services

The scope of the social services

The personal social services administered by local authorities cover a very wide spectrum, and they include important functions, such as education and housing, which are dealt with separately in this book. This chapter will confine itself to those social services which are within the ambit of the social service department of a local authority—i.e. for which the director of social services is responsible under the Local Authority Social Services Act, 1970. It is obviously not possible within the compass of a book of this size to detail all the multifarious services provided, but an attempt will be made to give a broad indication of those services which are considered to be of the greatest consequence to people in their daily lives.

The care of the poor, the aged and the handicapped

The Poor Law Act of 1601 (see Chapter 4), which provided for the relief of poverty as a legal obligation, may well be regarded as the foundation upon which our public social services have been built. The Poor Law Amendment Act, 1834, which transferred to elected boards of guardians responsibility for the relief of the destitute, was inspired by Jeremy Bentham, whose creative mind had been applied to the radical reform of public institutions, including the poor law. Bentham firmly believed in the principle of 'less eligibility'—i.e. that the lot of the pauper who applied for relief should be made more irksome than that of the labourer who contrived to maintain himself and his family without public aid. His view was that the able-bodied, instead of being granted outdoor relief, should be admitted to a well-regulated workhouse, where they would be taught to develop habits of industry and become useful members of society.

It gradually became evident, however, to the boards of guardians and to the central authority for poor law administration that the application of the principle of 'less eligibility' was very difficult in practice. By 1852 there were still 800 000 people in receipt of relief, and the paupers on outdoor relief outnumbered those accommodated in workhouses by seven to one. By the beginning of the twentieth century the harshness and severity of poor law administration had been considerably mitigated. Thus books, toys, tobacco and snuff were provided for workhouse inmates, and trained nurses and doctors were employed to look after the sick in poor law infirmaries. This policy was continued by the Local Government Act, 1929, which, in accordance with recommendations made by a Royal Commission in 1909, abolished the poor law guardians and transferred their functions to the county councils and county borough councils, each council working through a public assistance committee. The Act of 1929, although it did not achieve the final break-up of the poor law, provided that any functions of the public assistance committee might be performed by any other committee of the council, thus enabling many people who applied for relief to avoid the stigma of pauperism. Pauper children of school age, for example, could be dealt with by the education committee and the sick poor by the health committee.

The final destruction of the poor law was brought about by the National Assistance Act, 1948. The giving of relief in money or in kind is, in general, no longer the duty of local authorities: it is now the responsibility of the Department of Health and Social Security. The Act, however, required county councils and county borough councils to provide residential accommodation for persons who because of old age, infirmity or other circumstances were in need of care and attention, and to provide welfare services for blind, deaf, dumb and other handicapped persons. The same local authorities also had to provide temporary accommodation for people who were in urgent need of it as a result of fire, flooding, eviction or other unforeseen circumstances.

Some of the aged and infirm are still accommodated in former poor law establishments or in large private houses or hotels which were purchased by the local authority and adapted for use as houses for old people, but an increasing proportion of the accommodation now consists of purpose-built homes. Although there is a great diversity in the type of resident, ranging from the physically handicapped and infirm to the comparatively able-bodied, the majority of the people in these homes are not bedridden but may require some nursing care and attention. The local authority fixes a standard charge for accommodation based on the full cost, but relatively few residents pay the standard charge. They pay according to their means, some of them paying only the minimum weekly charge prescribed by the Department of Health and Social Security.

During the past two or three decades local authorities have considerably widened the scope of their activities in relation to old, infirm and handicapped people by providing, either directly or on an agency basis, services such as concessionary or free fares on 'buses, annual holidays at cheap rates, meals on wheels, mobile libraries, social clubs and day centres, and by making reduced charges for bowling and putting greens in the council's parks. The powers and duties of local authorities concerning disabled persons have been further extended by the Chronically Sick and Disabled Persons Act, 1970, which is dealt with later in this chapter.

The Seebohm Report

In 1965 a Committee under the chairmanship of Lord Seebohm was appointed to review the personal social services of local authorities. The Report of the Committee, which was issued in 1968, drew attention to the erratic course of the development of the social services, the inadequacies in the extent of provision, the lack of co-ordination between the various social agencies and the difficulties experienced by people in gaining access to the services provided. Different members of the same family, for example, might be visited within a very short period by a number of specialist social workers employed in different departments of the same local authority, each interested solely in one individual and in one aspect only of the social services. The Committee accordingly recommended that all major local authorities in England and Wales should establish a unified social service department with its own principal officer, who would report to a separate social services committee. The responsibility of the new department was to include the services then provided by children's departments, the welfare services provided under the National Assistance Act, 1948, the home help service, mental health social work services, adult training centres and day nurseries. The report met with a mixed reception. It proposed that the health services should remain outside the new department, but although there was considerable support for the view that health should not be separated from welfare, this view was not accepted.

The Local Authority Social Services Act, 1970

The substance of the Seebohm Report was embodied in the Local Authority Social Services Act, 1970, which unified the service without making any change in the local authorities administering it or any substantial change in the existing legislation. Under the Local Government Act, 1972, however, the responsible local authorities are now the non-metropolitan county councils and the metropolitan district councils. The Act of 1972 made no change in London, where the appropriate local authorities are the London borough councils and the City of London Corporation.

Each local authority is required to appoint a social services committee, which may include a minority of co-opted members. All matters relating to the authority's social service functions, except the levying of a rate or the raising of a loan, must be assigned to its social services committee, and unless the matter is urgent the authority may not exercise any of those functions without first considering a report from the committee. The functions of the main committee may be delegated to subcommittees.

Each local authority is also required to appoint a director of social services, and the Secretary of State for the Social Services may veto the appointment of any person he considers to be unfit for the post.

The functions within the ambit of the social services committee are set out in the Act of 1970. They include the care of the aged, the infirm and the handicapped, the care of deprived children, the supervision of child minders, the provision of day nurseries, the provision of home helps, and welfare functions relating to mental illness.

The care of children

Before the operation of the Children Act, 1948, which has been described as 'the children's charter', the law relating to the care and welfare of children was contained mainly in the Children and Young Persons Act, 1933. In 1945, however, public opinion was aroused by disclosures of unsatisfactory arrangements for the boarding out of children, and in consequence the Home Secretary appointed a Committee under the chairmanship of Miss Myra Curtis 'to inquire into existing methods of providing for children who from loss of parents or from any cause whatever are deprived of a normal home life'. The Children Act, 1948, implemented the main recommendations of the Curtis Report.

The Act of 1948 imposed on county councils and county borough councils the duty of taking care of children deprived of a normal home life. For this purpose each of these authorities was required to set up a children's committee to which the council might delegate any of its functions, except the levying of a rate or the raising of a loan. The committee was to include persons with experience in the care of children, but the majority of its members were to be members of the council.

Each county council and county borough council was to appoint a children's officer. Before making the appointment the local authority was required to submit to the Home Secretary particulars of the persons from whom it was proposed to make a selection, and the Home Secretary could prohibit the appointment of any applicant who was not considered by him to be a fit person.

The Act of 1948 imposed upon the local authorities the duty of receiving into their care any child in their area under the age of 17 who had no parent or guardian, or had been abandoned or lost, or whose parents or guardians were prevented by incapacity or any other circumstances from providing proper accommodation, maintenance or upbringing. They were also required to assume full responsibility for all children in need of care and protection who were committed to their care by a juvenile court.

The Curtis Committee had recommended that healthy children in the care of local authorities should be dealt with wherever possible by making arrangements for their adoption or, if this method was not available, by boarding out the children with private families. The Act of 1948, however, placed no emphasis on adoption, and in discharging their responsibilities local authorities provide and maintain children's homes, reception centres, residential nurseries and other residential establishments where children are looked after by staff employed by the council. In addition, some of the children in the care of the authority are accommodated in voluntary or private homes, and for others arrangements are made for adoption. The work of the council also includes the supervision of children under court orders. A high proportion of the children in the care of the authority are boarded out with foster-parents. Some difficulty is experienced in finding the right type of foster-parents. Efforts have been made by some local authorities to attract additional foster-parents by publicity, but offers from intending foster-parents are accepted only after their homes have been visited and inspected by the council's social workers, who satisfy themselves as to the suitability of the home environment before the child is finally placed. Throughout the period during which the child is boarded out, the home is visited periodically by the local authority's officers. The great majority of the children in the care of local authorities are boarded out or accommodated in council, voluntary or private homes. The average weekly cost of boarding out a child is only about a third of the cost of maintaining a child in a council home.

Children who cannot be boarded out are usually accommodated in homes maintained by local authorities or in homes run by voluntary bodies. In recent years there has been a general movement towards accommodating children in small homes in preference to larger homes with an institutional atmosphere. All voluntary and private homes accommodating children are inspected by the Department of Health and Social Security or by the local authority.

In the past, local authorities have maintained a variety of residential establishments for children, including children's homes, approved schools and remand homes. Under the Children and Young Persons Act, 1969, however, all these establishments have been replaced by 'community homes' provided by local authorities and voluntary bodies but planned on a regional basis.

The parents of a child who is in the care of a local authority are required to contribute according to their means towards the maintenance of the child until he attains the age of 16, and a child over 16 who is in remunerative full-time employment must himself contribute.

The Children and Young Persons Act, 1963, in placing emphasis on the preventive and rehabilitative work of local authorities, has imposed on them the duty of giving advice, guidance and assistance with the object of diminishing the need to receive children into care or to bring them before a juvenile court. In carrying out their duties under this Act local authorities are empowered to provide material assistance, including financial help, which cannot be obtained from other sources. Thus, heavy arrears of rent, rates and accounts for gas and electricity are sometimes paid to a parent, particularly if he has a large number of children, in the hope that this course of action will result in the family being preserved as a cohesive unit and that the children will not be received into care.

Day nurseries and child minders

Day nurseries should not be confused with nursery classes or nursery schools, which are run by local education authorities and have an educational rather than a social object. Under the National Health Service Act, 1946, it is the duty of the local authority to make arrangements for the care of children who have not attained the age of 5 and are not attending school. Admission to day nurseries, which are provided by both local authorities and voluntary bodies, is normally restricted to priority classes—e.g. where the mother is compelled to go out to work, to children of widows, to children of divorced or unmarried mothers, or to children of families where the home conditions are unsatisfactory from a health point of view. The hours of opening and closing the day nurseries enable the mother to escort her children to the nursery before she goes to work and to call for them after she has finished work. The charges made in council day nurseries are normally related to the means of the parent.

Under the Nurseries and Child Minders Regulation Act, 1948, as amended by the Health Services and Public Health Act, 1968, local authorities are required to keep registers of premises in their area where a child under 5 years of age is looked after for reward for an aggregate period of more than two hours per day. People who look after their close relatives do not have to register.

The home help service

Under the Health Services and Public Health Act, 1968, local authorities must provide a home help in a household where there is sickness or infirmity, for an expectant mother and in certain other specified circumstances. Reasonable charges may be recovered from the persons concerned, according to their means. The home help service has developed in various ways. Thus, some local authorities have provided family helps to take care of children in their own homes in cases where the mother has to go in to hospital for confinement or for an operation. Another development is a 'friendly neighbour' scheme, under which elderly people are helped by neighbours. For this service they are paid a flat rate instead of the hourly rate normally paid to home helps.

Mental illness and mental handicap

The first Act dealing with mental illness was passed in 1743. It provided that dangerous lunatics might, with the consent of the justices, be chained up. In 1808 the justices in Quarter Sessions were empowered to set up county lunatic asylums, and a further Act, passed in 1845, made it obligatory for Quarter Sessions to take care of paupers of unsound mind. The Local Government Act, 1888, placed upon county councils and county borough councils the responsibility for the care of the mentally unsound. The present law is contained in the Mental Health Act, 1959.

T–E

The Department of Health and Social Security is responsible for the central direction of the mental health services. The area health authorities are concerned with the treatment of mentally disordered persons in hospitals, and admissions to hospitals may now be arranged informally, in the same way as arrangements are made for the admission of patients who are suffering from other types of illness.

The mental health social workers, employed in the social service department of the local authority, deal with people of disordered mind who are in need of care and attention. The mental health social worker is the person to turn to for advice and support when any problems relating to mental disorder arise, and in certain circumstances he may arrange for compulsory admission to hospital. Local authorities may provide residential accommodation for the purpose of mental rehabilitation—e.g. after-care hostels, where patients provide for their own needs and go out to work, or fully staffed establishments providing residential care for people on their way back to normal life. Occupational therapy facilities are provided at day centres for people recovering from mental illness.

Mental handicap is sometimes confused with mental illness, but mental illness may respond to treatment and may sometimes be cured. Mental handicap, on the other hand, is not curable, though the development of mentally handicapped people can often be improved by education, training and social care. The care of the mentally handicapped is in the process of undergoing a complete change as a result of the new policy envisaged in a White Paper entitled *Better Services for the Mentally Handicapped* issued in 1971. The emphasis is placed in the White Paper on the mentally handicapped person living with his own family, but if he has to leave his family, unless he requires special medical treatment or nursing, the intention is that he should be looked after by foster-parents or go into a local authority home or hostel rather than into hospital. Responsibility for the education of mentally handicapped children is now the function of local education authorities, but local authorities who administer the Local Authority Social Services Act, 1970, provide adult training centres for persons over the age of 16, the aim of which is to offer an industrial form of training to assist them to take their places in outside industry.

The Chronically Sick and Disabled Persons Act, 1970

This Act, which has been described as a charter for the handicapped, requires the local authority to ascertain the people in its area who are handicapped by illness, injury, congenital deformity or old age so that the authority can provide the administrative machinery for dealing with their problems. The extent to which the Act has so far been implemented varies greatly from one area to another, and many of the services referred to in the Act were already being provided by some local authorities before the Act came into operation.

Help is given in innumerable ways. Thus, local authorities must ensure that at premises open to the public parking facilities and toilets are accessible to the disabled. Where necessary, a local authority is required to adapt a disabled person's home for his safety, comfort or convenience—e.g. by providing a ramp, a lift, or a ground-floor bathroom or lavatory. The authority must provide or make arrangements for people who are disabled to obtain radio or television sets. A telephone must be provided if the disabled person is living alone and one is not already within easy access. Meals must be supplied at home or at centres which the disabled person can attend, and holidays must be provided at holiday homes and elsewhere. The local authority may employ a voluntary organisation to undertake any of these services on its behalf, and in appropriate cases charges may be made according to means. One enterprising local authority has enlisted the services of 500 milkmen as 'front

line contacts' to alert the council's social workers when
speedy help is needed for old people suddenly stricken by
sickness or injury in the home.

Voluntary organisations

Voluntary bodies have played and are still playing a vital
part in the development and administration of the social
services. Frequently voluntary organisations have pioneered
successful social projects, which have later been put into
operation on a national scale by local authorities. A number
of statutes enable local authorities to work in co-operation
with local authorities and to contribute towards their
expenses. Thus, under the National Assistance Act, 1948, a
local authority may, in making arrangements for promoting
the welfare of blind, deaf, dumb or crippled persons, employ
as their agent a voluntary organisation. Under Part II of the
Children Act, 1948, children in the care of a local authority
may be placed in homes maintained by them or by voluntary organisations. A large number of children, for example,
are placed by local authorities in Dr Barnardo's Homes,
who make a charge to the local authority. In the field of
social service, grants are made by local authorities to such
organisations as citizens' advice bureaux, marriage guidance
councils, the Invalid Children's Aid Association, the
National Society for the Prevention of Cruelty to Children
and to voluntary bodies maintaining workrooms for the
elderly. Grants are also made by some local authorities
towards the expenses of a voluntary local council of social
service, which seeks to promote the formation of voluntary
organisations in the area, to publicise their work, to give
them advice and assistance, and to co-ordinate their
activities.

10   Health

Early health legislation

According to Disraeli, 'The health of the people is really the foundation upon which all their happiness and all their powers as a state depend.' Yet until the middle of the nineteenth century there was no strong conviction on the part of the governing classes that the health of the people was of direct concern to the state. Legislation of a piecemeal nature from the Middle Ages dealt with such questions as the disposal of rubbish and the drainage of land, but in a predominantly rural country co-ordinated action on a large scale to improve the health of the community was considered unnecessary. When the impact of the Industrial Revolution began to make itself felt, however, and congestion and squalid living conditions in the large towns which sprang up rapidly in the Midlands, Lancashire and Yorkshire produced outbreaks of cholera, the legislature was compelled to turn its attention to concerted measures for the prevention of disease.

There is little doubt that progress in the field of public health received a powerful impetus from cholera. Cholera was the most dependable ally of Edwin Chadwick (1800–90), the champion of the public health movement, in the protracted battle he waged against vested interests in squalor and filth, who stubbornly resisted every attempt on his part to develop a sanitary code.

Although *ad hoc* local authorities to deal with the paving, lighting and cleansing of the streets and with the prevention of nuisances had been established from about 1750 onwards in many large towns, and the functions of some of these bodies included the levelling and widening of streets and the supply of water, they were incapable of coping with the first of the cholera outbreaks which occurred in 1831–2. The Privy Council, therefore, in 1831 set up a Central Board of Health, which was empowered to issue proclamations and establish temporary local boards of health in urban areas, but when the outbreak of cholera subsided no further action was taken.

On the passing of the Poor Law Amendment Act, 1834, Chadwick, a disciple of Jeremy Bentham (1748–1832), the great reformer, was appointed Secretary of the Poor Law Commissioners; but Chadwick's main interests were in the field of public health rather than in the relief of the destitute. An administrative genius with the zeal of an enthusiastic missionary, he was strongly imbued with the desire to make sweeping reforms in the public health system. He was, however, tactless and uncompromising, and, as an ardent exponent of central control over local authorities, he encountered strong opposition from those who regarded him as a dangerous bureaucrat. In 1836 Chadwick was instrumental in persuading Parliament to pass an Act creating a General Register Office for the purpose of registering births, deaths and marriages. The Act provided for the appointment of a General Registrar and for local registrars to be appointed by the local boards of guardians. With the help of statistics obtained from the registrars relating to mortality rates and diseases, Chadwick began his campaign. In 1838 he submitted a report to the Home Office, showing that in London there was a close relationship between the small sum of money devoted to the relief of the poor and the failure of the Government to deal with insanitary conditions. This report was followed in 1842 by the issue of a comprehensive report by the Poor Law Commissioners, covering the whole country, which drew further attention to the deplorable sanitary conditions revealed by their investigations. More copies of this report (which was written mainly by Chadwick) were sold by the Stationery Office than of any previous Government publication, but legislation was delayed pending the appointment of a Royal Commission. The Report of this Royal Commission, which was issued in 1845, confirmed the conclusions of the Poor Law Commissioners. The Report recommended that full-time district medical officers should be appointed; that drainage, the cleansing and repair of streets, and water supply should be under one authority in each area; and that the central government should be empowered to compel a recalcitrant local authority to carry out its duties.

No immediate action was taken, but the spread of cholera on the Continent during 1847[1] emphasised the need for early legislation. The Public Health Act, 1848, provided for the setting up, for a period of five years, of a General Board of Health, consisting of the President and two other persons appointed by the Crown. This General Board of Health was empowered to create in each locality a local board of health either on receipt of a petition signed by at least one-tenth of the ratepayers or, if no petition was received, where the death rate was at least twenty-three per thousand. The local board of health in a borough was to be the borough council, and elsewhere it was to be an entirely new authority, its members being elected by plural voting. Each local board was required to appoint a clerk, a surveyor and an inspector of nuisances, but the appointment of a medical officer of health was optional. The functions of the local board included water supply, sewerage, drainage, the repair and cleansing of streets, the prevention of nuisances, the disposal of refuse, the provision of sanitary conveniences, the registration of slaughter houses and common lodging houses, the regulation of buildings and offensive trades, and the provision of burial grounds. Expenditure on these

[1] This epidemic did not reach Britain until October 1848.

services could be defrayed out of a rate levied by the local board. The central control of the local boards by the General Board of Health—which took the form of audit of accounts, inspection by the General Board's inspectors and the right of the General Board to veto the appointment of an inspector of nuisances—was in conformity with Chadwick's cherished ideas on centralisation; and as a member of the new General Board, Chadwick was given an opportunity of shaping its policy. But Chadwick, in his anxiety to make rapid headway, paid little heed to the prevailing distrust of bureaucratic control, with the result that the General Board of Health was dissolved on the expiry of the term of five years for which it had been set up, and thereafter the Board survived only on a year-to-year basis until its demise in 1858.

The reaction against bureaucracy found expression in the Local Government Act, 1858, which transferred the functions of the General Board of Health to the Home Office and the Privy Council. Henceforth a locality could not be compelled to set up a local board of health: the establishment of such a board in any area was to be on a purely voluntary basis. But a further outbreak of cholera in 1866, though of moderate dimensions in comparison with those of previous outbreaks, once again drew attention to sanitary deficiencies and led in 1868 to the appointment of a Royal Sanitary Commission. The Report of this body, which was issued in 1871, contained the following recommendations:

1 That in urban areas sanitary functions should be the responsibility of a single authority—in boroughs the borough council and elsewhere a local board of health.
2 That in rural areas the board of guardians should be the sanitary authority.[1]
3 That a central authority with supervisory powers over

[1] The boards of guardians, which had been set up under the Poor Law Amendment Act, 1834, had already acquired experience of sanitary functions in administering the Nuisance Removal Acts, 1846 to 1866.

both poor law and public health should be appointed with power to compel a locality to adopt the sanitary code.

The substance of these recommendations was embodied in the Local Government Board Act, 1871, and the Public Health Act, 1872. The Act of 1871 created the Local Government Board, which was given jurisdiction over all local authorities concerned with sanitation and poor law administration, whilst the remaining recommendations of the Royal Commission were embodied in the Act of 1872. This Act, together with further sanitary legislation, was, however, repealed and consolidated by the Public Health Act, 1875, which remained the foundation of the law relating to sanitation and cognate matters until the passing of the Public Health Act, 1936, now the basis of the present law. The Local Government Board remained the controlling authority over poor law administration and public health until 1919, when it was superseded by the Ministry of Health.

A wider conception of responsibility

The recommendations of the Royal Sanitary Commission (1868–71), although at that time regarded as enlightened and far-reaching in their scope, were concerned largely with environmental public health services. The vision of the Commissioners hardly extended beyond the narrow confines of refuse removal, drainage, water supply and other services necessary to prevent the recurrence of large-scale epidemics. Since the last quarter of the nineteenth century, however, the state and local authorities have developed a far wider conception of responsibility for the health of the people: attention has been focused not only on the importance of the environmental services, which in recent years have received increasing attention, but also on health services of a personal nature. This wider conception of responsibility found expression, as far as local authorities were concerned, in legislation relating to the housing of the working classes (now for all classes of the population), the direct treatment of disease in public hospitals, the medical inspection and treatment of school children, the provision of domiciliary nursing and midwifery services, family planning, and the care of mothers and young children, culminating in the National Health Service Act, 1946, and the National Health Service Reorganisation Act, 1973, under which a comprehensive health service has been established.

The development of municipal hospitals

The Public Health Act, 1875, enabled local authorities to provide hospitals, but very few local authorities availed themselves of this power. The Isolation Hospitals Acts, 1893 and 1901, empowered county councils to provide hospitals for persons suffering from infectious diseases, and, in the meantime, infirmaries for the destitute sick were being set up in large numbers by boards of guardians. The standards of nursing and medical attention in these infirmaries were at first very low, but conditions gradually improved. The Local Government Act, 1929, transferred the functions of the boards of guardians, including their hospital services, to county councils and county borough councils, and the same Act empowered these authorities to provide general hospitals and to formulate schemes for the provision of hospitals for infectious diseases. From 1930 onwards county councils and county borough councils converted many of the old infirmaries into modern hospitals, and some new hospitals were built. Although the standards of the municipal hospitals in some areas were very high, the hospitals throughout the country were unevenly distributed, and the service suffered from lack of co-ordination.

The administrative structure before the 1974 reorganisation

The National Health Service Reorganisation Act, 1973, reformed the structure of the National Health Service on a unified basis with effect from 1 April 1974. Before that date the health of the people was the joint responsibility of the central government and local authorities, but some of the most important personal health services were not the direct concern of local authorities. Briefly, the division of responsibility was as follows:

(a) *The central government*

The Department of Health and Social Security supervised the hospital services. The country was divided into fifteen regions, each of which had a Regional Hospital Board, the members of which were appointed by the Secretary of State for Social Services. The hospitals formerly administered by local authorities had been taken over in 1948, when the National Health Service Act, 1946, came into operation. The Regional Hospital Boards had an overall responsibility to the Department of Health for the hospitals (except the teaching hospitals) in their region, but the day-to-day administration was left to Hospital Management Committees, the members of which were appointed by the Regional Hospital Boards. Both the Regional Hospital Boards and the Hospital Management Committees were required to include persons appointed after consultation with the local health authorities. Each Hospital Management Committee was usually entrusted with the management of a group of hospitals. Each teaching hospital—i.e. a hospital which shared with a university the task of training doctors and dentists—had its own Board of Governors, appointed by the Secretary of State for Social Services.

Doctors, dentists, chemists and opticians who decided to work in the National Health Service were under the jurisdiction of the local executive council. The executive council was not a local authority, but there was usually an executive council for the area of each local health authority—i.e. for each county and county borough. The members of the executive council were appointed by professional organisations, the Department of Health and Social Security, and the local health authority. All the services mentioned above were financed nationally.

(b) Local authorities

The environmental health services provided by local authorities—e.g. sanitation, smoke control, refuse collection and building regulation—were normally the responsibility of county borough, non-country borough, urban district and rural district councils. The personal health services—e.g. the provision of ante-natal and post-natal clinics, the supervision of midwives and health visitors, home nursing, family planning, vaccination and immunisation, health centres, and the ambulance service—were administered by the local health authorities (i.e. the county councils and county borough councils). In London, the London borough councils and the City of London Corporation were responsible for both the personal and the environmental health services. The medical inspection and treatment of school children were administered by the local education authority, which was usually also the local health authority.

The personal health services mentioned above were administered by the local health authorities, mainly in accordance with the provisions of the National Health Service Act, 1946, The local health authority had to appoint a statutory committee, known as the health committee, a majority of whose members were required to be members of the authority.

The responsibilities of the local health authority included the care of expectant and nursing mothers, and for this purpose they made arrangements for the provision of ante-natal and post-natal clinics, and of child welfare centres where advice was given on hygiene, feeding, etc., and welfare foods were supplied at reduced charges. Under the Midwives Acts and the Act of 1946, local health authorities were required to arrange for a domiciliary service of mid-wives, who could be employed either directly by the local authority or by voluntary organisations or hospitals; and under the Act of 1946, health visitors employed by the authority were required to visit homes in their area to give advice on the care of young children, to persons suffering from illness and to expectant and nursing mothers. Local health authorities were also required to provide nurses to attend on persons who needed nursing in their own homes, and arrangements were sometimes made for lending sick-room equipment without charge to the patient. The functions of the local health authority also included family planning. The National Health Service (Family Planning) Act, 1967, empowered local authorities to make arrangements for giving advice on contraception and for the supply of contraceptive substances and appliances.

Although vaccination was no longer compulsory, local health authorities were required to make the necessary arrangements for vaccination against smallpox and the immunisation of children against diphtheria. Some local health authorities also provided immunisation against whooping-cough and tetanus. All local health authorities made arrangements for vaccination against poliomyelitis.

The National Health Service Act, 1946, provided for the setting up of health centres—i.e. premises for the accommodation of a group of doctors and dentists, and for pharmaceutical services and all the services provided by a local health authority. The authority was required to provide, equip and maintain the premises, and to provide the staff, with the exception of medical and dental staff. By the time the local health authorities relinquished their control more than 400 health centres were functioning, but at some of these centres not all the services envisaged in the Act were provided.

Local health authorities also had the duty of providing ambulances for conveying to hospital persons suffering from illness or mental disorder, or expectant or nursing mothers who were unfit to travel by other means. These ambulances could be provided either by the authority itself or by voluntary organisations. In London responsibility for this service rested with the Greater London Council.

The present administrative structure

The National Health Service Reorganisation Act, 1973, gave effect to the proposals contained in two White Papers —one for England and the other for Wales—issued in 1972. The Act brought under unified administration (i) the hospital services previously administered by Regional Hospital Boards, Hospital Management Committees and Boards of Governors of teaching hospitals; (ii) the functions of the National Health Service executive councils; (iii) the personal health services formerly administered by local health authorities; and (iv) the school health service. Personal health services are now outside the sphere of local government, but local authorities retain responsibility for the environmental health services, which are summarised later in this chapter.

The new integrated administrative structure for the personal health services came into operation on 1 April 1974. Central responsibility rests with the Department of Health and Social Security, in England, but fourteen Regional Health Authorities, consisting of members appointed by the Secretary of State, are responsible for strategic planning. The pivot of the new structure is, however, the Area Health Authority, which consists of members appointed by the Regional Health Authority and not less than four members appointed by the corresponding local authority. Outside London the boundaries of the Area Health Authority coincide with those of the non-metropolitan counties and metropolitan districts, and in London there are in most cases groupings (normally of two or three London boroughs) for each Area Health Authority. Within the area of each Area

Health Authority there are one to five districts, and in each district there is a Community Health Council, not less than half of whose members must be appointed by local authorities in the district. The functions of the members of the Community Health Councils are to represent the interests of the public and to monitor the effectiveness of the Area Health Authority. Provision is also made for the appointment of Health Service Commissioners for England and Wales to investigate complaints. It will be seen that, although the personal health services previously administered by local authorities are no longer their responsibility, a link with local government is retained by ensuring that the boundaries of the new local government areas coincide with those of local authorities, and that some of the members of the Area Health Authorities and Community Health Councils are appointed by local authorities.

The environmental services

The local authorities now responsible for the administration of the environmental health services are normally the councils of metropolitan and non-metropolitan districts. In London the local authorities are the councils of the London boroughs and the City of London Corporation. Most of the environmental health functions of local authorities are derived from the Public Health Act, 1936, but since that date important additional powers and duties have been acquired by various statutes. An indication is given below of the main services which local authorities administer.

1   *Sanitation*

Before the coming into operation on 1 April 1974 of the Water Act, 1973, it was the duty of the local authority to provide such public sewers as might be necessary for draining the area and to arrange for the disposal of the sewage. These sewers belonged to and were maintained by the local authority, but the drains by which each individual building was connected with the sewers were in private ownership, and where the existing drainage arrangements were inadequate the owner of the property might be required at his own expense to connect his drains to the local authority's sewers. The local authorities were the borough, urban and rural district councils and, in London, the London borough councils and the City of London Corporation. The Greater London Council was responsible for main drainage. Under the Water Act, 1973, however, ten regional water authorities have been established in England and Wales, and some of their members are appointed by local authorities. Statutory responsibility for sewerage has been transferred to these regional authorities, who have other important functions, including the prevention of river pollution and water supply; but provision is made in the Act for the discharge of sewerage and other functions on behalf of the regional water authority by the new local authorities responsible for environmental health. For the time being, local authorities are acting as agents for some of the functions of these regional authorities, but not for sewage disposal. Local authorities retain drainage functions (as opposed to sewerage functions) in their own right.

2 *Abatement of nuisances*

The local authority is required to inspect its area for the detection of statutory nuisances and to serve an 'abatement notice' on an offender, requiring him to abate the nuisance. If he does not comply with the notice, legal proceedings may be instituted by the local authority in a magistrates' court, and the court may make a 'nuisance order' requiring the abatement of the nuisance and the execution of any necessary works. There is a right of appeal against a nuisance order to the Crown Court. Nuisances cover a wide range of matters involving the health and comfort of the community —e.g. the accumulation of deposits of filth, carrying on offensive trades, allowing trees to overhang on public highways and excessive noise.

3 *Removal and disposal of refuse etc.*

The cleansing of streets and the removal of house refuse are included in the duties of local authorities, and the county council is responsible for refuse disposal. The removal of trade refuse may be undertaken at a reasonable charge. Under the Civic Amenities Act, 1967, county councils are required to provide refuse dumps for bulky rubbish, including old cars, free of charge to residents.

4 *Provision of sanitary conveniences*

Local authorities may provide public conveniences and may make bylaws regulating their use.

5 *Regulation of buildings*

Local authorities regulate the construction and height of buildings, their lighting, ventilation and drainage, and the provision of sanitary conveniences in buildings in accordance with building regulations made by the Department of the Environment.

6 *Infectious diseases*

Certain types of infectious disease—e.g. smallpox, cholera, typhus and poliomyelitis—must be notified to the appropriate authority by the doctor in attendance. The purpose of notification is to enable the authority to take steps to control the spread of infection, and the local authority may, in certain circumstances, order the disinfection of a house or, in default, undertake the work itself. Since the reorganisation of the National Health Service on 1 April 1974, Area Health Authorities have appointed officers with medical qualifications who have assumed responsibility for infectious disease and food poisoning control and act in an advisory capacity to the local authority in other aspects of environmental health.

7 *Parks and open spaces*

Under the Public Health Acts local authorities may provide parks and pleasure grounds. These powers were

T–F

considerably extended by the Open Spaces Act, 1906, which conferred powers on local authorities, which are now exercised by the Greater London Council, county and district councils, London borough councils, and parish and community councils. Portions of the grounds may be appropriated for games, and entertainments may be provided.

8   *Unsound food*

The Food and Drugs Act, 1955, enables an authorised officer of a local authority—e.g. a public health inspector—to inspect food which is exposed for sale, or which has been sold, and to take away samples of such food for examination by the local authority's analyst. The sale of food which is deficient or injurious to health renders the vendor liable to prosecution.

9   *Smoke control*

The Great Smog of 1952, which is said to have caused 4000 deaths, led to the setting up of the Beaver Committee on Air Pollution, and the Clean Air Act of 1956 was based on its recommendations. Under the Clean Air Acts, 1956 to 1968, local authorities may by order, on confirmation by the Secretary of State for the Environment, declare the whole or any part of their area to be a smoke control area. In these areas the emission of smoke caused by the use of unauthorised fuel is an offence, and fireplaces must either be adapted to burn smokeless fuel or not used at all. As a result of these measures, there has been a considerable improvement in the atmosphere, especially in London. Smoke in the air has been reduced to between a third and a quarter of that prevailing ten years ago, and there has been no London smog since 1952.

The protection of the environment

In recent years there has been an increasing awareness of the evils of pollution and of the need to protect the environment. In many countries, particularly the USA where pressure groups have been very active, a great deal of interest has been shown in environmental problems, and there has been deep concern about the extinction of many species of plant and animal life. Matters relating to the human environment were discussed at a United Nations Conference held for this purpose in Stockholm in 1972, when world attention was focused on environmental problems. This Conference was attended by 1200 delegates from 110 countries. In this country heavier penalties have been prescribed in recent Acts of Parliament—e.g. under the Deposit of Poisonous Waste Act, 1972, and the raising in 1971 of the maximum fine for the illegal discharge of oil to £50 000. Much of the legislation relating to pollution and the protection of the environment is enforceable by local authorities. Unfortunately, one of the main difficulties associated with the protection and improvement of the environment is the fact that more prudent care for environmental consequences, which is advocated by the conservationists, is frequently incompatible with the exploitation of natural resources and the promotion of industrial growth.

11 Housing

Nineteenth-century legislation

During the first half of the nineteenth-century, when the Industrial Revolution was transforming large portions of rural England into urban areas, it was necessary for homes to be built in large numbers to meet the needs of the rapidly growing population. The artisans and their families who flocked to the towns to secure employment in the new industries were housed in dwellings provided by private builders. As these houses were erected for workmen of limited means, and as minimum standards of construction were not prescribed by the legislature, the houses were built very badly and often lacked those public services which today would be regarded as essential. They were built as close as possible to one another (sometimes back to back) and without drains, piped water supply or privies.

The first enactment to improve the standard of housing took the form of a permissive Act, which was passed in 1851. The Shaftesbury Act of that year enabled borough councils and local boards of health to provide lodging houses for the working classes. In the meantime the Public Health Acts, which were passed from 1848 onwards, by regulating the construction of new buildings and insisting on minimum requirements of sanitation in existing buildings, attacked the root causes of bad housing. The Shaftesbury Act, 1851, was followed by the Torrens Act (Artisans' and Labourers' Dwellings Act), 1856, which imposed upon the owner the responsibility of keeping a house in good condition, and by the Cross Act, 1875, which empowered local authorities to demolish slum areas. Following the report of a Royal Commission which was set up in 1884 to inquire into the housing conditions of the working classes, a comprehensive Act—the Housing of the Working Classes Act, 1890—was passed dealing with the clearance of slum areas, improvements to individual houses and the building of new houses of a higher standard. This Act was known as the 'Principal Act' until 1925.

The Housing Act, 1957

Most of the present law in relation to the housing functions of local authorities is now to be found in the Housing Act, 1957, and in subsequent legislation. A highly controversial enactment passed by the Conservative Government (the Housing Finance Act, 1972) made changes of a very substantial nature, particularly with regard to rents chargeable in both the public and the private sectors, but this Act is likely to be repealed by the Labour Government, which assumed the reins of power in March, 1974.

Under the Local Government Act, 1972, the local authorities for housing outside London are the metropolitan and non-metropolitan district councils, and in London, the Greater London Council, the London borough councils and the City of London Corporation. The GLC administers the larger housing estates, and the London borough councils and the City are concerned with the smaller estates and with unfit individual houses. County councils are not normally housing authorities, but in exceptional circumstances a county council may, with the consent of the Secretary of State for the Environment, exercise certain reserve powers.

The Act of 1957 deals with (i) unfit individual houses, (ii) the clearance and redevelopment of insanitary areas,

(iii) overcrowding and (iv) the provision of new houses.

Unfit individual houses

If a house is considered by the local housing authority to be unfit for human habitation and can be rendered habitable at a reasonable cost, the local authority may serve a notice on the owner requiring him to carry out the necessary repairs within a stipulated time, and if he does not comply the local authority may do the work and recover the cost. The owner has the right to appeal to the County Court.

If, however, the local authority is satisfied that the house cannot be repaired at a reasonable cost, and the owner fails to execute the necessary repairs, the local authority must make a demolition order, requiring the house to be demolished, and if this order is not obeyed the local authority may itself demolish the house and recover the cost from the owner. It sometimes happens that only part of a dwelling—e.g. the basement—is unfit for habitation and the remainder of the house is habitable. In such cases the local authority, instead of making a demolition order, must make a closing order, prohibiting the use of that part of the house which is unfit, except for a purpose approved by the local authority. Where a demolition or closing order is made by a local authority, the owner of the house concerned has the right to appeal to the County Court.

Clearance of insanitary areas

If a whole area is considered to be insanitary, the local authority can pass a resolution declaring the area to be a 'clearance area'. The clearance area must be defined on a map and a copy of the local authority's resolution must be forwarded to the Secretary of State for the Environment. In implementing its resolution the local authority can now no longer make a clearance order, requiring the owners to demolish the buildings, but must make a compulsory purchase order, in which case the local authority purchases the area and itself demolishes the buildings. Having made the compulsory purchase order, the local authority advertises the making of the order and serves notices on the interested persons. The order requires the confirmation of the Secretary of State, and if objections are received within a prescribed period he must hold a public local inquiry before he reaches a decision.

In 1972 the Minister for Housing predicted that, with the increase in the Government slum clearance subsidy to 75% of expenditure, all the slums in the country would be cleared by 1980, but the indications now are that this forecast was unduly optimistic. On the other hand, in a report issued at about the same time by Shelter, the housing and poverty action group, the gloomy prognostication was made that at the existing rate of progress it would take as long as 204 years.

General improvement areas

Sometimes a predominantly residential area, although badly in need of attention, does not require clearance but can be dealt with less drastically by restoration and the creation of a more pleasing appearance. In such cases the local authority may, under the Housing Act, 1969, declare the area to be a 'general improvement area'. If it is decided to improve the general quality of the environment in this way, the local authority, having passed a resolution to that effect, acquires the land by agreement or (with the approval of the Secretary of State) compulsorily and then proceeds to carry out the necessary works with financial assistance from the Government.

Overcrowding and under-occupation

The average number of persons per household in Great Britain is about 2·7, and even in London, where overcrowding is particularly acute, the position is not significantly different. In theory, therefore, there should be no over-crowding, but owing to the unevenness of distribution the true situation presents an intractable problem for many local authorities, especially in the densely populated sectors of large cities.

Local authorities have a duty to inspect their areas with a view to ascertaining the extent to which overcrowding exists and to take steps to abate it. The Housing Act, 1957, defines overcrowding in some detail. If, for example, two or more people over the age of 10 of opposite sexes and not living together as husband and wife, sleep in the same room, that room is deemed to be overcrowded. A child under the age of 12 months is not taken into account, but a child over that age but under 10 years is reckoned as half a unit. Under the Housing Acts, 1961 and 1969, local authorities have special powers to deal with overcrowding in houses in multiple occupation. The authority may fix a limit to the number of people who can live in a house, and after the issue of such a directive the owner or occupier may not allow more people to move in if the limit has already been reached. Although legal proceedings may be taken against a person who permits overcrowding, the practical problems of rehousing have impeded rapid progress in some of the most congested areas.

Closely allied to the problem of rehousing is that of underoccupation. There is, of course, a great deal of underoccupation in owner-occupied homes, but there are also many council houses and flats which provide accommodation for tenants far in excess of their needs. There are, for example, numerous cases of middle-aged and elderly couples whose children have married and have set up separate homes living in, say, a three-bedroomed house. Having established roots in the area, they are naturally reluctant to leave their home, despite the fact that the accommodation they occupy exceeds their requirements and smaller accommodation would be less costly. If these tenants could be induced to move to, say, a one-bedroomed flat, the vacated accommodation could be released for families with children who have been on the council's waiting list for many years and are in desperate need of a home. Other action which might make a useful, if only a marginal, contribution to the solution of the housing problem would be the abolition by all local authorities of their remaining restrictions on council tenants taking lodgers.

Compensation

If a house is unfit for human habitation, the amount of compensation normally payable to the owner is the value of the site cleared of buildings, but an additional payment may be made if the property has been well maintained. The local authority may make a contribution towards the occupier's removal expenses and, if he carried on a trade or business in the house, towards his loss from disturbance to that trade or business. Compensation at a higher rate is payable to owner-occupiers of unfit houses, provided that certain conditions are fulfilled. When a site is acquired by a local authority for a statutory purpose either compulsorily or by agreement—e.g. for road widening or for the building of a new school—compensation at the full market rate is paid for any property on that site which is in a satisfactory condition.

The Land Compensation Act, 1973, provides for the payment of compensation to the owner of residential property where the value of his interest is depreciated by certain physical factors, such as noise, dust, vibration, smell or fumes arising from works to highways, aerodromes, etc., carried out under statutory powers. For the first time compensation is payable to people whose property has not been acquired by the local authority but, because it is in close proximity to large-scale construction or demolition by a local authority, has in some way been injuriously affected. There are also home loss payments of up to £1500 for people, even if they are furnished tenants, who are displaced from their homes in which they have lived for at least five years and which have been purchased compulsorily by the local authority.

Under the Act of 1973 local authorities are under a duty to provide suitable alternative accommodation for people who are forced to move from their homes as the result of a demolition order, a closing order or a compulsory purchase order. The obligation to rehouse is, however, discharged by the offer of a mortgage advance.

The provision of new houses

Even before 1914 there was an acute shortage of houses for the working classes. Although the sanitary requirements imposed by the Public Health Acts did much to improve the standard of housing, they inevitably raised the cost, with the result that only the better-paid artisans could afford to rent the houses built by local authorities and philanthropic organisations. The cessation of house-building during the First World War and the shortage of labour and materials which followed it aggravated the difficult situation. In 1919, therefore, the Government found it necessary, in order to cope with the unprecedented demand for houses, to grant subsidies to local authorities and private builders for the erection of new houses, and from 1921 onwards grants were made to local authorities for slum clearance. About 4 000 000 houses and flats were built in England and Wales between 1919 and 1939. About 2 900 000 of these were built by private enterprise with or without a Government subsidy, and the remaining 1 100 000 by local authorities with Government assistance.

When the Second World War ended in 1945 the shortage of houses was more serious than it had ever been before, as during the War building was at a standstill and there was widespread damage and destruction of houses by enemy action. Owing to the high cost of labour and materials, the Government, in order to stimulate the building of houses, had no alternative but to make grants to local authorities on a much more generous scale than before the War. As a result of this policy, there was an almost continuous increase in the rate of house-building, which rose to over 400 000 annually. Some of these houses and flats were built by local authorities with the aid of a Government subsidy and others by private enterprise. Since the Housing Act, 1949, local authorities have been empowered to provide houses not only for the working classes but for all classes of the population regardless of means, and some of the dwellings constructed by local authorities are of a high standard. Amenities sometimes include central heating, double glazing and waste disposal units, and some of the larger houses and flats have two bathrooms. In the early 1970s however, owing to difficulties experienced by intending purchasers in obtaining mortgages, steep rises in rates of interest and alarming increases in the cost of land and various other factors, house-building by both local authorities and private builders suffered a serious decline, falling to less than 300 000 in 1973, with the result that there is now an acute shortage of accommodation—particularly for newly weds wishing to set up a home—and a disquieting increase in the number of homeless families.

Homeless families

The plight of homeless families poses an intractable problem for local authorities, particularly in the more densely populated parts of London and other large industrial cities. There is no doubt that many people have become homeless through no fault of their own, and they are deserving of the unstinted help of local authorities. The most common cause of homelessness was the eviction of tenants by private landlords from furnished rented accommodation, as until recently furnished tenants had very limited security of tenure. Families in this category are in the last resort provided with temporary accommodation (frequently of substandard quality and with shared bathroom and kitchen facilities) by local authorities. But, unfortunately, there are some homeless people who are feckless and irresponsible, and who place undue reliance on the beneficence of the Welfare State, making little or no effort to help themselves. Many tenants have been evicted by private landlords or local authorities for persistent failure to pay rent. Even when, after eviction, they are provided with temporary accommodation by the local authority at a very moderate weekly charge, it is frequently found that they build up further heavy arrears. Some local authorities, in an effort to discharge their responsibilities, have purchased premises for housing homeless families and have, in addition, provided bed-and-breakfast accommodation in hotels at great expense to the ratepayer. One of the many problems facing local authorities is that the more sympathetic the approach to homeless people arriving from other areas, the greater is the number of homeless they have to accommodate in their own area. On the other hand, if they adopt a policy which is lacking in compassion, they may have to take children into care in council homes at even heavier expense to the local ratepayer. In addition, the children are then separated from their parents and there is a break-up of the family, a situation which local authorities should do their utmost to avoid. The problems of the homeless have to some extent been mitigated by the Rent Act, 1974, which gave security of tenure to furnished tenants where the landlord is not resident on the premises. It would appear, however, that this new legislation may have added to the difficulties experienced by tenants in finding suitable furnished accommodation. It is noteworthy that the Francis Committee (1971), after considering this matter at some length, had recommended with only one dissentient voice that furnished tenants should not be given unlimited security of tenure. Incidentally, a laudable achievement in which local authorities participated was the absorption in 1972 of a large number of Asian refugees from Uganda, 14 000 of the 28 000 refugees having been settled in local authority housing in 300 areas.

The selection of council tenants

There are in Great Britain nearly twenty million dwellings. More than half these are owner-occupied, and of the remainder almost six million—i.e. approximately 30%—are occupied by council tenants. The great majority of the balance of four million dwellings are owned by private landlords or by housing associations, which are non-profit-making voluntary organisations providing homes for the elderly and various other classes of persons, with assistance from public funds. Almost all the houses and flats in the private sector—i.e. those owned by private landlords— have their rents controlled or regulated by legislation.

In dealing with applications for council housing accommodation, local authorities are required to give preference to persons who are occupying insanitary or overcrowded houses and to those who have large families. Some local authorities allocate houses on a points system, those applicants with the highest number of points being allotted accommodation as it becomes available. The practice adopted by some local authorities of insisting that the applicant must have resided in the area for a specified period before his name is placed on the waiting list has been condemned in reports on the selection of tenants issued from time to time by the Government. Although it is the natural wish of a local authority to safeguard the interests of its residents of long standing, such a policy tends to be parochial in its outlook. It restricts movement of population at a time of less than full employment, when mobility of labour should be encouraged in the national interest. Many local authorities are also faced with the difficult question of occupational preference. In some areas there is an acute shortage of teachers, firemen, public health inspectors, planners and social workers, and frequently it is impossible for the authority to fill vacant positions without offering council housing accommodation in the area. There are also in some areas numerous vacancies for other essential jobs— e.g. for police, nurses and midwives—which may not be directly concerned with local government. Many local authorities, however, whilst recognising the vital importance of filling these vacancies, are loath to depart from the principle of selecting tenants on the basis of the greatest housing need.

The fixing of rents

For many years the general rule was that local authorities could charge such reasonable rents as they thought fit. During the latter part of the tenure of office of the Labour Government (1964–70), however, local authorities were precluded from raising council rents by more than a moderate weekly sum annually, and when the Conservatives came into power in 1970 they passed the Housing Finance Act, 1972, which virtually removed from local authorities the power to fix the rents of council dwellings. This new legislation established bodies known as Rent Scrutiny Boards, whose members were appointed by the Government, and they were empowered to determine 'fair rents' for all council dwellings on the same basis as the rents which were being dealt with by rent officers in the private sector. 'Fair rents' are, in effect, market rents less a deduction for scarcity of accommodation in the area. The Act of 1972 introduced a new rent rebate scheme on a national basis, which enabled a high proportion of council tenants, subject to a means test, to claim rent rebates on a fairly generous scale. A council tenant, for example, with an average industrial wage who has a wife (not working) and two dependent children would, if asked to pay a 'fair rent' of, say, £7 a week exclusive of rates, be entitled to a rent rebate, and if his earnings are below the national average his rebate could be very substantial. Local authorities may, at their discretion, increase rebates subject to an overall 'tolerance' of 10%, but if they do this the excess expenditure must be defrayed from local rates and not from the National Exchequer, which reimburses local authorities the greater part of the cost of rent rebates. The Housing Finance Act, 1972, also introduced a scheme of rent allowances in the private sector on lines similar to the national rent rebate scheme, but despite widespread publicity comparatively few tenants of private landlords have availed themselves of this facility. Although there are many tenants who complain bitterly of increases in prices of food and who protest with vehemence at higher fares, for some reason best known to themselves they will not take the trouble to complete a claim form to obtain a sizeable rent allowance from their local authority. On returning to office in March 1974, the Labour Government announced their intention to repeal the Housing Finance Act, to which they had from its inception been vigorously opposed.

The sale of council houses

In the past, successive Conservative governments have encouraged the sale of council houses, and in pursuance of this policy the Minister of Housing and Local Government and later the Secretary of State for the Environment issued circulars giving general consent to the sale by local authorities of houses to sitting tenants and to other persons in need of accommodation. In 1968, however, the Labour Government changed this policy, and local authorities in London and other large cities were not permitted to sell each year more than one in every 400 houses which they owned. This decision was justified by the Government on the ground that extensive use by local authorities of the power of sale would eventually result in a serious depletion in the stock of houses available for letting to persons in need. When these restrictions were lifted by the Conservative Government, which came into office in 1970, some local authorities offered council tenancies for sale at prices of up to 30% lower than the current market price, but in return for this concession the purchaser was not permitted for a period of five years to resell the house without giving the council the first option to repurchase.

Loans for house purchase

Under the Housing (Financial Provisions) Act, 1958, local authorities (i.e. district councils, county councils, London borough councils and the Greater London Council) are empowered to advance money to enable a person to purchase a house or a flat. It is the normal practice to restrict advances to residents within the area of the authority who wish to purchase a dwelling in the area or within a short distance of its boundaries. The loan, which is no longer limited by statute to a percentage of the local authority's valuation (it may be as high as 95% or even 100%), can be made on dwellings irrespective of their value, but local authorities normally have a price limit. The rate of interest charged to borrowers is at the discretion of the local authority.

The number of loans granted for house purchase by local authorities is small in relation to the number of advances by building societies. Building society mortgages represent about 90% of the total, whilst local authority mortgages account for only about 5%. Nevertheless, local authorities provide a very useful social service, as they normally lend a higher percentage of the cost of a house than a building society would contemplate and they lend money on older properties on which building societies are very reluctant to make advances. Moreover, some local authorities, in an effort to provide the utmost assistance to intending purchasers of moderate means, including young married couples, grant loans to two or even three joint mortgagors and allow the prospective purchasers to undertake heavy monthly commitments, particularly if they are in a position to provide a guarantor for the repayments.

Grants for improvement

The purpose of these grants is to assist owners of old houses which still have a useful life to bring them up to date and to provide modern amenities. The local authorities concerned are the district councils and, in London, the London borough councils and the City of London Corporation. The two most important types of grant are intermediate grants for the provision of standard amenities—e.g. a fixed bath, a sink, a wash-basin or a hot and cold water supply—and improvement grants, which are wider in their scope and include alterations and enlargements.

Under the Housing Act, 1974, the maximum grant for each standard amenity has been greatly increased—e.g. to £100 for a fixed bath, shower or sink and there have also been increases for improvement grants. Further increases in the maximum improvement grants have been made by departmental order. The normal limit for a dwelling is now £3200, but a grant of up to £3700 may be made for the conversion of a three-storey dwelling. Areas with special housing and social problems, known as 'housing action areas', will be designated, and in these areas the maximum grant will be 75% of the cost of the work, and as high as 90% where hardship is involved. In 'general improvement areas', which are predominantly residential in character, where shopping precincts, gardens and other general amenities may be provided, the maximum grant is 60%, and in any other area 50%. Improvement grants are payable for repairs and replacements as well as for improvements. In addition to intermediate and improvement grants, special grants are payable by local authorities for improvements to houses in multiple occupation.

12   Town and Country Planning

The object of planning

The object of planning is to ensure that all land is put to the use which is best from the point of view of the community. Before the advent of town and country planning, when building was left to the unrestrained initiative of individual landowners, the development of land was promiscuous and unco-ordinated. Although bylaws relating to building dealt with safety, light and ventilation, they were not concerned with the orderly development of large areas. Such questions as the adequacy of playing fields and swimming pools, the mingling of factories and dwellings, facilities for transport and amusement, and the preservation of buildings of architectural, historic or artistic interest were not the concern of any public authority. The price of neglect is being paid today, and will continue to be paid for many generations to come.

Garden cities

The earliest efforts to regulate development took the form of garden cities, which were the work of private enterprise. Following the publication of a book by Ebenezer Howard in 1898, in which he advocated the creation of garden cities, a limited liability company, called the Garden City Ltd, was formed with the object of putting Howard's ideas into practice, and in 1903 the Letchworth estate in Herts was purchased for development as a garden city. Letchworth was laid out on model lines, and in 1920 Welwyn (Herts) was developed on the same principles.

The creation of garden cities has not been confined to private enterprise. Manchester City Council has created Wythenshawe, and Liverpool City Council is responsible for a similar venture at Speke, but neither of these two satellite towns meets the requirements of a true garden city as they are close to their parent cities and too closely linked with them.

Town-planning legislation

The earliest town-planning legislation was associated with housing. The first Act dealing with town planning—the Housing, Town Planning, etc., Act, 1909—authorised the council of any county borough, borough or district to prepare a town-planning scheme, but any scheme submitted was to apply only to land in course of development or which appeared likely to be used for building purposes— i.e. it was not to include land already built upon. The Housing, Town Planning, etc., Act, 1919, required urban authorities with a population of more than 20 000 to prepare schemes, and the Local Government Board, which at that time was the central authority responsible for town planning, was empowered to require any local authority to prepare a scheme. The first Act dealing solely with town planning was the Town Planning Act, 1925, which consolidated previous legislation and gave local authorities additional powers. In recognition of the fact that the areas of some local authorities might be too small for town-planning purposes, the Local Government Act, 1929, provided that a town-planning scheme could be prepared by the county council, acting in conjunction with the borough or district council. Legislation was consolidated in the Town and Country Planning Act, 1932, which provided that, in future, schemes might be prepared for any type of land, whether urban or rural and whether built upon or not.

Despite all this legislation, by 1939 only about 5% of England and Wales was covered by planning schemes. The large number of small separate planning authorities, the expense of paying heavy compensation to landowners and the complicated administrative machinery all played their part in retarding progress. But during the Second World War (1939–45) serious attention was focused on the problem of making planning legislation more effective. The Report of the Royal Commission on the Distribution of the Industrial Population (the Barlow Report), which was issued in 1940, emphasised the need for positive action in regard to planning in order to ensure the proper distribution of industry, and the Town and Country Planning Act, 1944, dealt with the rebuilding of blitzed areas. Meanwhile, the importance attached to planning was emphasised by the creation in 1943 of a Ministry of Town and Country Planning to supervise and co-ordinate the work of local planning authorities. The efforts of the legislature to plan the use of land culminated in the Town and Country Planning Act, 1947. The then Minister of Town and Country Planning, Mr Lewis Silkin, when he introduced the Town and Country Planning Bill in the House of Commons, described it as 'the most comprehensive and far-reaching measure ever placed before the House'. Most of the provisions of this Act, however, have since been repealed and incorporated in the Town and Country Planning Act, 1971. There have also been changes in the authorities responsible for planning (Local Government Act, 1972) and in compensation (Land Compensation Act, 1973).

Planning authorities

The central authority is the Department of the Environment (formerly it was the Ministry of Housing and Local Government), and until 1 April 1974 the local planning authorities were the county councils and county borough councils, but provision was made for the delegation by county councils of some planning functions to county districts—i.e. to the second-tier authorities. The planning position in London, which was not affected by the Local Government Act, 1972, is dealt with in Chapter 20. County districts with a population of more than 60 000 could claim delegation of certain planning functions—e.g. applications for planning permission, tree-preservation orders and the control of outdoor advertising—and the Department of the Environment could authorise similar delegation to a county district with a population of less than 60 000. All this, however, has been changed by the Local Government Act, 1972, which came into operation on 1 April 1974 and confers planning powers on both the new first- and second-tier types of authorities—i.e. on county councils and district councils.

Development plans

Briefly, the division of responsibility for development plans is that the county council (whether metropolitan or non-metropolitan), after consulting the district councils in its area, prepares the structure plan and, in doing so, takes into account such matters as the resources of the area, employment prospects, cultural and educational facilities, and traffic problems. After objections to the structure plan have been heard by the Secretary of State for the Environment, he confirms it (with or without modifications) or rejects it. The preparation of local plans, which must not be in conflict with the structure plan, is the responsibility of the district authority, but although objections must be given full consideration local plans are not subject to the approval of the Secretary of State.

Control of development

Applications for development cover a very wide range. There may, for example, be an application for consent to erect a large office block or a shopping centre with several storeys of residential accommodation above. On the other hand, local authorities also have to deal with numerous applications of a minor character, such as extensions to individual houses or the conversion of an existing house to two or three self-contained flats. Prior permission in all these cases must be obtained from the local planning authority, which is normally the district council. If, however, the application relates to a county matter—e.g. a departure from the structure plan—the decision will rest with the county council. The Local Government Act, 1972, places an obligation on a planning authority, if so requested by a parish council, to inform that council of every planning application likely to affect the parish.

An applicant who is dissatisfied with a local authority's decision regarding an application for development has a right of appeal to the Secretary of State for the Environment. Some appeals are decided by the Secretary of State on the basis of written representations by both parties, but where the application is of a more contentious nature an inquiry is held in public by one of the Department's inspectors before a decision is reached. In some cases the final decision rests with the inspector who conducted the inquiry. In only about 10% of the appeals is the decision of the Department in conflict with that of the local authority; and another deterrent to appeal, apart from the possible expense, is the fact that it normally takes several months, and sometimes as long as a year, before an appeal is heard and the decision is notified to the appellant.

Public participation

In recent years increasing interest has been shown in public participation in local government, particularly in relation to planning. In some areas neighbourhood councils have been formed to act as an antidote to apathy and as a forum for local involvement in public affairs, and the declared aim of the Association for Neighbourhood Councils, which was formed in 1970, was to establish 'parish councils within towns'. In the field of planning, an important development was the publication in 1969 of a report entitled *People and Planning* (the Skeffington Report). Its terms of reference were to 'consult and report on the best methods, including publicity, of securing the participation of the public at the formative stage in the making of development plans for their areas'. Consultation and co-operation at all times is, however, not always a realistic ambition. The wider the public involvement in a major planning decision, the greater is the risk of protracted progress and indecisive results. It is interesting to note that when the Greater London Development Plan was published in 1970 there were as many as 21 000 objections. However laudable public participation may be in the interests of the grass roots of democracy, it undoubtedly gives rise to considerable procedural and practical problems.

Public participation in planning does not extend to the right of a third party to appeal against an individual planning decision in which he has no legal interest. If, for example, a person owns a house adjoining a property which is the subject of a planning application for an extension, the owner of the house may object to the proposal if he has been made aware of it, but he has no right of appeal to the Department of the Environment if planning permission is granted by the local authority.

Compensation for compulsory acquisition

The subject of compensation has already been dealt with in Chapter 11, but a problem which is frequently encountered by owners when large-scale redevelopment is contemplated by a local authority is that of planning blight.

If, for example, a local authority were to consider the widening of a main thoroughfare or the building of a new road, involving the demolition of privately owned property in the area, the owners affected would find it difficult, if not impossible, to dispose of their property at a reasonable price whilst the matter was under consideration, and the uncertainty might go on for several years, in which case the owners might be involved in serious financial hardship. It has for a long time been possible for the owners of the property concerned to serve a blight notice on the local authority, requiring the authority to purchase the property. Now, under the Land Compensation Act, 1973, it is no longer necessary for an owner to wait until a compulsory purchase order has been confirmed, and the position of owners affected by blight is generally more favourable than it was under previous legislation.

Town development

A method of providing for the decentralisation of population and industry was provided by the Town Development Act, 1952. The object of the New Towns Act, 1946, was to relieve overcrowding by the creation of new towns, but the Town Development Act, 1952, aimed at achieving this object by assisting local authorities who undertake smaller schemes to expand existing centres of population. Schemes may include shopping centres and factories as well as housing. The Act has met with only limited success, but the London County Council (and later the Greater London Council) has made arrangements with a number of local authorities who have indicated their willingness to take some of London's surplus population. The expanding towns enter into an agreement with the GLC providing for financial assistance to the receiving authority, and the GLC has the right to nominate as tenants London families wishing to move out to one of these towns.

Green belts

The Ministry of Housing and Local Government and the Secretary of State for the Environment have from time to time issued circulars to local authorities on the subject of the preservation of extensive open spaces, drawing their attention to the importance of checking the unrestricted sprawl of built-up areas. Local planning authorities have been urged to designate green belts several miles around built-up areas. Under the Green Belt (London and Home Counties) Act, 1938, local authorities are empowered to prevent buildings from being erected on certain open spaces surrounding London. The green belt is a stretch of about 840 square miles of open country encircling London's built-up area. Ministers have repeatedly emphasised that, whatever demands are made by industry, housing, motorways and water supplies, the Government is determined to adhere in substance to the green-belt policy. The total amount of land in England subject to green-belt policies of all kinds is 5600 square miles.

13 Public Security

The voluntary police system

In a civilised community the primary duty of the Government is to maintain law and order and to protect life and property. During the Middle Ages law enforcement was dealt with at first under the frankpledge system (Chapter 1) and later by unpaid parish constables working under the direction of the local justices of the peace. Whilst the country was rural in character, the maintenance of public security and the suppression of crime presented no insuperable difficulties to the parish organisation, which sufficed more or less to meet the needs of the situation, but even in Tudor times the maintenance of order in London was a problem of some magnitude. The narrow streets and cellar-dwellings afforded sanctuary for murderers, robbers and other malefactors, and the paid watchmen who were supposed to patrol the streets at night proved largely ineffective. In the reign of Charles I more night watchmen (known as 'Charlies') were appointed, but their unreliability was so notorious that the practice of wealthy merchants and other persons of affluence of employing private bodyguards became more prevalent. During the eighteenth century the increase in the amount of wealth—especially of movable property—the increase in the popularity of travel and the corruptness of some of the justices of the peace, known as 'trading justices', all played their part in the creation of a wave of crime, particularly in the more populous areas.

In London the spread of crime and disorder was, however, arrested in 1748, when Henry Fielding, the novelist, was appointed magistrate to preside at Bow Street Court. During Fielding's period of office (1748–54) the administration of justice was put on a more efficient and impartial basis. Fielding organised a small band of paid policemen, later known as the 'Bow Street runners', who achieved some success in tracking down criminals and in making London safer for the law-abiding citizen. The 'Bow Street runners' were at first upright and honest men, but later they succumbed to corrupt influences and their standard of efficiency deteriorated. From time to time the London mob took full control of the metropolis, the most destructive outbreak of mob violence, known as the Gordon riots, occurring in 1780. Lord George Gordon, the leader of the mob, organised huge processions of Protestants, who marched through the city, burning and looting public buildings and the houses of Catholics. For several days London was at the mercy of the rioters, but apart from the use of troops the Government had no means at its disposal of restoring order. A similar outbreak took place at Birmingham in 1791, and the Luddite Riots of 1811–12, which occurred in various parts of the country and involved the destruction of vast quantities of valuable machinery, demonstrated the inability of troops to combat disorders of this type. The failure of military force as a means of coping with orderly processions was shown even more forcibly at the Peterloo Massacre of 1819, when a body of Yeomanry attacked with drawn sabres a peaceful gathering of textile workers, killing eleven and wounding several hundred.

In attempting to suppress crime and disorder without the aid of an efficient police force, the courts inflicted ruthless punishment on offenders. By 1800 the number of felonies punishable by death reached a total of 253. The theft of any article of the value of more than 5s. was a capital offence, and even children were hanged for stealing. Convicted criminals were executed publicly at Tyburn and elsewhere. The severity of sentences which could be imposed on offenders frequently made juries unwilling to convict accused persons, with the result that sometimes criminals whose guilt was firmly established were acquitted. Most of these inhuman penalties were, however, removed by Sir Robert Peel (Home Secretary 1822–7) and by the Judgment of Death Act, 1836, which greatly reduced the number of capital offences.

At the end of the eighteenth century it had become manifest that the parochial police system was totally incapable of dealing with the new conditions which had arisen as a result of the Industrial Revolution. In many of the larger towns *ad hoc* local authorities, known as improvement commissioners or police commissioners, had been set up to deal with the problem, and in some urban areas, including London, watchmen were employed to patrol the streets at night; but piecemeal measures of this type achieved little success. An attempt was made by William Pitt in 1785 to pass into law a Police Bill, under which paid police officers, under the control of salaried magistrates, would be responsible for law and order in the City of London and in Westminster and Southwark. Opposition was, however, voiced by the City of London Corporation, and, moreover, it was felt that the sacrifice of liberty involved in submitting to a paid police force would be too high a price to pay for security from crime. As a result the Bill was withdrawn.

Sir Robert Peel, on becoming Home Secretary in 1822, set up a committee on police reform. The committee reported that in their view freedom and an effective police system were incompatible, but Peel's retort was that 'liberty does not consist in having your house robbed by organised gangs of thieves'.

The establishment of the Metropolitan Police

Sir Robert Peel's Metropolitan Police Act, 1829, passed through Parliament without opposition and almost without debate. The new paid police force was to operate in the Metropolitan area (excluding the area of the City of London) and was to be under the control of two Commissioners who would work under directions from the Home Secretary.

At first the new police were very unpopular. They were unfairly criticised in the press and by the general public, and assaults on policemen were overlooked by magistrates or dealt with in lenient fashion. A baton charge against a London mob in 1833 evoked violent accusations of police brutality, despite the fact that in this conflict it was the police who suffered the greater number of serious casualties. Gradually, however, a more friendly relationship developed between the police and the general public, and before many years had elapsed the institution of an effective police system had been justified.

The establishment of police forces in the boroughs and counties

The improved arrangements for policing the metropolis drew attention to the serious deficiencies in the arrangements elsewhere, and when the Municipal Corporations Act, 1835, reformed the boroughs the opportunity was taken of making the borough council responsible through its watch committee for the control of a paid police force.

The setting up of police forces in London and in the boroughs paved the way for the extension of the system to the counties. The police organisation in the counties was still based on the parish constables, of whom there were one or more for each parish. Even if these constables had been efficient, the area of the parish was far too small for them to function effectively. The existence of forces in the metropolis and in the boroughs, which were gradually increasing in efficiency, created the risk that criminals might migrate to the county areas unless they, too, were made part of a satisfactory police system, particularly since the advent of the railways, which facilitated rapid movement. Moreover, Chartist disorders, which occurred in 1839, emphasised the need for the creation of an efficient police force covering the remainder of the country.

The County Police Act, 1839, was a permissive Act. It enabled the justices in Quarter Sessions to raise and equip a paid police force out of the rates. The same year saw the establishment by local Act of a paid police force in the City of London, replacing the out-of-date force of watchmen and beadles. But by 1856 there were still twenty counties in which a paid police force had not been set up, the reluctance to adopt the Act being on grounds of expense to the ratepayers.

The County and Borough Police Act, 1856, compelled the justices in Quarter Sessions to establish a paid police force for each county, and went some way to meet the objections of those counties who had not yet set up a police force by making a grant of one-quarter of the cost of pay and clothing of borough and county police forces which were certified by a Home Office inspector to be efficient. It is significant that, despite the long-standing tradition of independence of municipal corporations, both the borough and county forces were henceforth to be subject to central inspection.

With the advent of the motor car it became clear that small isolated police forces would not be able to cope with highly mobile criminals. As the criminal mind pays no respect to obsolete administrative boundaries, the area of administration for police purposes has been gradually widened, and after the passing of the Police Act, 1946, the police authorities outside the Metropolitan Police District (an area somewhat larger than that of Greater London) were normally the county and the county borough. Further changes were made by the Police Act, 1964, and from that date amalgamations of police forces, resulting in a substantial reduction in their number, were made by the Home

Secretary in the interests of the efficiency of the service. The Act of 1964 was amended by the Local Government Act, 1972, to take account of the new structure of local government.

The police forces today
The different types of police forces are now as follows:

1   *The county police*
From the coming into operation of the Local Government Act, 1888, until 1964, the police functions formerly exercised by the justices in Quarter Sessions were the responsibility in each county of a standing joint committee, consisting of equal numbers of county justices, appointed by Quarter Sessions, and members of the county council. The standing joint committee indented on the county council for its expenses, and the county council had to comply with its demands. The Police Act, 1964, however, replaced the standing joint committee by the police committee. Two-thirds of the members of this committee now consist of members of the county council and one-third of magistrates.

2   *Combined police forces*
A combined police force may have been established as the result of either a voluntary or a compulsory amalgamation. If two or more police forces wish to amalgamate, they must submit an amalgamation scheme to the Home Secretary for his approval. If the Home Secretary wishes to create a combined police force by compulsory amalgamation, he must, unless the police authorities concerned are in agreement, hold a local inquiry before making an order, which is laid before Parliament. When a combined police authority is set up, two-thirds of its members are members of the constituent councils and one-third are magistrates for the constituent areas. Its finances are raised by precepts—i.e. demands for money to cover its expenses—on its constituent councils.

3   *The Metropolitan Police*

This force is under the direct control of the Commissioner of Police of the Metropolis, who is appointed by the Crown on the recommendation of the Home Secretary. The Metropolitan Police District, which covers an area of 786 square miles, is larger than the area of 610 square miles administered by the Greater London Council. Although the force is under national control, it is financed partly by local rates. In addition to the Government grant of 50% of expenditure, which is given to other police forces, the Treasury makes a special grant to meet the cost of national and imperial services, including the protection of the Royal Family and Ministers.

4   *The City of London Police*

This force, which was established in 1839 and operates in the square mile of the City, is controlled by the City of London Corporation.

Central control of police

Under the Police Act, 1964, the Home Secretary may make regulations as to the government, mutual aid, pay, allowances, clothing, expenses and conditions of service of the police, and every police authority must comply with these regulations. The appointment of a chief constable is subject to the Home Secretary's approval, and any member of a police force who is dismissed, or required to resign, or reduced in rank or pay is entitled to appeal to the Home Secretary. All police forces, with the exception of the Metropolitan Police, are open to inspection by Home Office inspectors, and the Government grant of 50% of approved police expenditure may be withheld by the Home Secretary if he is not satisfied that the force is being maintained efficiently. The City of London police grant is at the rate of one-third (not 50%) of its approved expenditure.

Special types of police

Women were first employed on police duties in the First World War. The prejudice against the employment of women as police officers has been largely overcome, and they are now employed by all police authorities. Women police have rendered valuable service, particularly in the field of juvenile delinquency.

Under the Police Act, 1964, special constables, with all the powers and responsibilities of the regular police, may be appointed by the Chief Officer of Police for the area to supplement the normal police services.

Railway and canal authorities have obtained powers under special Acts of Parliament to appoint police officers with limited jurisdiction.

Under the Road Traffic Regulation Act, 1967, police authorities may supplement the regular police forces by the appointment of traffic wardens to lighten the burden of the police in controlling and regulating traffic, especially in the parking of motor vehicles.

Fire authorities

Before 1938 local authorities, except the London County Council, had no legal obligation to provide a fire brigade. Optional powers were available in rural areas under the Lighting and Watching Act, 1833, which might be adopted by rural parishes, and in urban areas fire brigades might be provided under the Public Health Act, 1875. The Fire Brigades Act, 1938, however, made it compulsory for the councils of county boroughs, boroughs, and urban and rural districts to provide an efficient fire service in their area. In 1941, following widespread air attacks, the maintenance of the fire services was transferred to the National Fire Service, which operated under the direction of the Home Secretary, but the Fire Services Act, 1947, again imposed the duty of fire protection on local authorities.

T–H

Under the Local Government Act, 1972, the local authorities for fire protection are now the metropolitan and non-metropolitan county councils, but as in the case of the police, voluntary or compulsory amalgamation schemes may be made, with the approval of the Home Secretary, for the establishment of combined fire authorities. Fire authorities are required to co-operate with one another by making reinforcement schemes for mutual assistance.

Fire prevention

The Offices, Shops and Railway Premises Act, 1963, requires the local fire authority to deal with applications for fire certificates in the premises to which the Act relates, and provides for an appeal to a magistrates' court if a certificate is refused.

The most recent legislation relating to fire protection is the Fire Precautions Act, 1971, which applies to a wide variety of premises and particularly to hotels and guest houses. Although there are heavy penalties for failure to apply for fire certificates, progress in implementing this Act has been slow, and it will take many years before all the premises have been inspected and fire certificates have been granted. The fact that every year there are 900 hotel fires in which about twenty people die testifies to the highly unsatisfactory nature of the present situation, and in the interests of public safety there is an imperative need to bring the Act into full operation as speedily as possible.

14 Municipal Trading and Enterprise

The selection of services for municipal trading

Municipal trading services may be defined as those services on which the local authority hopes to make a profit or to run without loss. There are many services administered by local authorities—e.g. housing and baths—the receipts from which are substantial, but as these services are not intended to be self-supporting they are usually considered to be outside the sphere of municipal trading.

Certain services have been selected by the legislature as being suitable for municipal trading, whilst others have been rejected; and before dealing with the scope and variety of municipal trading services it would be well to examine the factors which are taken into consideration in determining the suitability of a service for municipal enterprise. It has been suggested that services are chosen on grounds of essentiality. Most of the municipal trading services are essential in character, but there are many essential functions —e.g. the supply of coal, food and clothing—which are normally outside the scope of municipal activity. Another feature of municipal trading is that a large amount of capital is usually required to start the enterprise—e.g. for establishing an aerodrome or a transport system—but this is not necessarily so: the setting up of a civic restaurant, for example, might not entail a large capital outlay. Generally speaking, it is true to say that the commodity or facilities provided by the municipality involve little or no question of individual taste or preference and are not subject to the vagaries of unpredictable changes in design or fashion: it is perhaps for this reason that local authorities have not undertaken the supply of clothing. A local monopoly is not an essential feature of municipal trading. Although competition with private enterprise may be wasteful and uneconomic, and many of the trading undertakings of local authorities are monopolies, there are some municipal services, such as civic restaurants and transport services, which have faced competition from local commercial interests.

Advantages and disadvantages

It is claimed that profits made by municipally operated undertakings are used in reducing the rates or in extending or improving the service, in which case the entire locality derives benefit, whereas in the case of private firms or public companies a portion of the profits might be used to increase the dividends of a limited number of shareholders. The most profitable municipal trading services, however, were those concerned with the supply of electricity, and as electricity supply is no longer a local authority function the amount of profit from municipal trading services which is applied to rate relief is now negligible. Some trading services, such as water supply, which is no longer a local authority function, rarely operated at a profit. It is also contended that local authorities derive some advantage from the fact that, in establishing or extending a trading service, they may be able to borrow money at a somewhat cheaper rate than that available to a private trader. Furthermore, the argument is adduced by the supporters of municipal enterprise that when experimental work is found to be necessary it is not discouraged by the fear that the expenditure to be incurred will make inroads on the dividends of shareholders.

Opponents of the extension of municipal trading activity contend that, by diffusing its energies over a wider field, the local authority may seriously impair the efficiency of its non-trading services; that the procedure of a local authority, with its necessity for committee approval of all major proposals, is unsuited to the management of a business enterprise requiring quick decisions on matters of policy; and that because the profit motive is not so strong as it is in private enterprise, municipal trading services cannot operate as efficiently or as economically as those run by a commercial organisation.

Scope and variety

Before the Second World War the most important municipal trading services were the supply of gas, water and electricity, and the maintenance of transport undertakings and markets. The Electricity Act, 1947, transferred the electricity functions of local authorities to the British Electricity Authority, and the Gas Act, 1948, transferred the gas undertakings of local authorities to Area Gas Boards. Since the War, however, local authorities have acquired new powers, notably in relation to civic restaurants, aerodromes and entertainments.

The wide variety of municipal enterprise is illustrated by the following examples: Birmingham has a municipal bank, and in 1968 the Corporation obtained powers to subsidise the rents payable by tenants to private landlords. On the coming into operation of the Housing (Finance) Act, 1972, this power became a duty, which was applied to all local housing authorities. Sheffield has a printing works which undertakes the printing required by the municipality. Hull operates a telephone service, which is the only exception to the monopoly of the Post Office in the field of telecommunications. Bradford provides a testing service for all textiles from original fibre to finished products. Harrogate owned Turkish baths, Colchester owns an oyster fishery, and Doncaster and Chester own race courses. A number of local authorities own golf courses, and others provide district heating facilities. Private Bills have been introduced by local authorities to ban the parking of heavy vehicles in residential streets.

Proposals made in 1948 by Coventry Corporation to operate radio stations, to run a taxi-service and to provide hotels were rejected by the electorate, and were not included in the Corporation Parliamentary Bill. At about the same time, Birmingham Corporation resolved to seek powers to run hotels, but this proposal was rejected by the electorate. Early in 1969 Parliament rejected Greater London Council proposals for the promotion of a municipal lottery and the setting up of a local radio station. A similar fate befell the Manchester Corporation (Lotteries) Bill in 1971.

A number of local authorities, particularly the large ones, have set up supplies departments for central purchasing, which enable the departments of the council to place requisitions with the chief supplies officer or to order what they require from the suppliers direct, in accordance with agreed arrangements. By purchasing supplies in bulk, local authorities (sometimes acting jointly) may obtain a substantial discount. General recognition of these powers has been given in the Local Authorities (Goods and Services) Act, 1970, which enables local authorities to co-operate with one another on a large scale not only in relation to central purchasing but also for sharing a computer and for providing administrative, technical and professional services. In recent years a number of local authorities have obtained powers to microfilm documents and to destroy the originals, thus saving valuable storage space. Some local authorities operate their own insurance schemes. Instead of insuring with insurance companies, they pay premiums into a special fund of their own and meet claims when received.

Under the Housing Act, 1947, local authorities are empowered to sell furniture or supply it on hire purchase to council tenants.

Transport undertakings

Local authorities first became responsible for transport undertakings in 1870, when the Tramways Act of that year enabled them to acquire the interests of private companies compulsorily or by agreement. At first the actual operation and management of tramways were left in the hands of the companies, to whom the tramways were leased at an annual rent, but later local authorities were allowed to operate their own undertakings. Before long the tramways faced serious competition from motor-buses, and some local authorities obtained power by local Act to run omnibus services themselves. Some local authorities (now district councils) still run bus services, but under the Transport Act, 1968, and the Local Government Act, 1972, each metropolitan county council is now a passenger transport authority, which decides matters of broad policy and finance but leaves day-to-day management to a largely autonomous body known as a passenger transport executive, consisting of a director general and a number of other salaried members appointed by the passenger transport authority. Outside the six metropolitan counties, however, district councils providing bus services must operate them in accordance with the general policy laid down by the county council, and both county and district councils may contribute towards the cost of public transport in their area.

The Civil Aviation Act, 1949, empowered county borough, borough and urban district councils, with the consent of the Minister of Aviation, to provide and operate municipal aerodromes, and a number of local authorities availed themselves of this power. A considerable number of aerodromes are now owned by local authorities—i.e. district councils—and some are operated by the authorities themselves.

Markets

The ownership of markets is the oldest form of municipal trading, and it is now the most profitable type of enterprise undertaken by local authorities. The Food and Drugs Act, 1955, empowered county borough, borough, and urban and (with the approval of the Minister of Housing and Local Government) rural district councils to acquire or establish markets, but most local authorities who own or control markets derive their powers from a charter or grant from the Crown or from a local Act of Parliament. The local authority may collect from persons using the market tolls, rents and stallages for the right to sell goods in the market-place or for setting up a stall there. Under the Local Government Act, 1972, the appropriate local authorities are the district councils and the London borough councils.

Water supply

Although water supply is not normally a profit-making service and is closely related to public health, it was generally included in the municipal trading services.

Until about the middle of the nineteenth century, water supply was controlled by private companies who charged excessive prices, with the result that only the upper classes could afford to pay for piped supplies of water, the poorer people being charged exorbitant prices for water obtained from standpipes and wells. These companies, who usually enjoyed a local monopoly, frequently supplied impure water, which caused serious outbreaks of cholera. Under the Public Health Act, 1848, local boards of health[1] were empowered to supply water, but in those cases where there was already a private water undertaking in existence the local authority was not allowed to provide water without the consent of the water company. The Public Health Act, 1872, for the first time imposed upon local authorities a

[1] See Chapter 10.

definite obligation to ensure adequate supplies, and these provisions were later embodied in the Public Health Act, 1936. The local authorities concerned were normally the councils of county boroughs, boroughs and urban and rural districts. Joint boards and joint committees for water supply were, however, formed under the Public Health Act, 1936, and some local authorities obtained powers by local Act or provisional order to supply water for catchment areas which bore little relation to local administrative boundaries. Charges for water for domestic purposes were generally made in the form of water rates, based on the rateable value of the premises.

The Water Act, 1945, provided that it shall be the duty of the Minister of Health (now the Secretary of State for the Environment) 'to promote the conservation and proper use of water resources and the provision of water supplies in England and Wales and to secure the effective execution by water undertakers, under his control and direction of a national policy relating to water'. This Act gave the Minister wide powers of co-ordination, including the amalgamation, compulsorily or by agreement, of two or more water undertakers, whether they were local authorities or water companies.

Water supply is no longer a local authority service. The Water Act, 1973, imposed on the Secretary of State for the Environment an overall responsibility for the conservation, augmentation, distribution and proper use of water resources, and the provision of water supplies. Nine regional water authorities have been established in England and the National Water Development Authority for Wales. These authorities are responsible not only for water supply but for other services, including sewerage and sewage disposal and the prevention of river pollution. Each water authority consists of a chairman appointed by the Secretary of State and of other members, some of whom are appointed by local authorities.

Restaurants

British restaurants (some of which were run by local authorities) were set up during the Second World War to provide additional communal feeding centres for blitzed areas. The cost of adaptation or construction of the premises and the cost of initial equipment were borne by the Ministry of Food. In 1943 there were over 2000 British restaurants serving about 500 000 meals daily.

The Civic Restaurants Act, 1947, enabled local authorities to continue on a permanent basis the restaurant services which were provided during the War. The Act empowered local authorities to establish and carry on restaurants, and, in addition to supplying meals and refreshments, to provide incidental and ancillary facilities. The local authorities with powers were normally county borough councils and county district councils. Some local authorities carried on their civic restaurants in conjunction with the school meals services. All the London County Council restaurants were closed in 1954 as they continued to show a deficit for several years, and the number of civic restaurants outside London is now negligible.

Entertainments

The Public Health Acts (Amendment) Act, 1907, enabled county borough, borough and district councils to provide band performances in parks or pleasure grounds. The Public Health Act, 1925, extended the entertainment powers of local authorities. Any enclosure set apart for bands might be used for concerts or other entertainments. Where the council themselves provided the entertainment, however, they were not allowed to produce a stage play or a variety performance; they were not permitted to use scenery or theatrical costumes; and no cinematograph films could be shown except those illustrative of questions relating to health or disease. Many local authorities obtained powers under local Acts to provide performances in any place of public resort in their area—i.e. even though not a park or a pleasure ground. These powers enabled municipal orchestras to be provided, especially at holiday resorts.

The Local Government Act, 1948, opened a very wide field of municipal activity in relation to the provision of entertainment and the development of cultural facilities. Under this Act the councils of county boroughs, county districts and London boroughs, and the City of London Corporation could provide or contribute towards the cost of entertainment of any kind, including plays, concerts, music and dancing. Expenditure was limited to a rate of 6*d.* in the pound plus the net receipts, but most local authorities spent only a small fraction of this amount. In pursuance of these powers, a number of local authorities operate municipal theatres or rent theatres to professional companies, whilst others give financial assistance to repertory theatres or to local amateur societies. Manchester City Council has assisted the Hallé Orchestra, and the Greater London Council has given grants to Sadler's Wells. Other local authorities have municipal symphony orchestras, and the London Borough of Croydon provides for a large catchment area a wide range of entertainment at Fairfield Halls, which comprise a concert hall, a theatre and a banqueting hall. The Greater London Council, which is the foremost local government patron of the arts in the country, runs the Royal Festival Hall and the Queen Elizabeth Hall, and is contributing to the cost of building a National Theatre.

Under the Local Government Act, 1972, the powers of local authorities in relation to entertainment have been extended to include all local authorities, including county councils and parish councils, and the financial limitations contained in the Local Government Act, 1948, have been removed.

15 Highways, Bridges and Rivers

The parish as highway authority

From Tudor times until almost the close of the nineteenth century the repair of highways was a parochial responsibility. The Highways Act, 1555, required the parish constables and churchwardens to call a meeting of the parishioners every year to elect two surveyors of highways, whose duty it would be to arrange for the repair of the highways in the parish. The surveyor, who received no remuneration for his services and was frequently totally unsuited to his onerous task, had to arrange for the farmers to provide carts, horses and oxen, and for the labourers in the parish to do four days a year (increased to six days by an Act of 1662) 'statute labour' in repairing the roads. Statute labour was unpaid, and it was the duty of the surveyor to levy fines on defaulters and to collect commutation money from those parishioners who preferred to make annual payments in lieu of rendering personal service.

Under the Highways Act, 1691, the justices of each petty sessional division of the county were required to hold special Highways Sessions for the transaction of highway business. The Act provided that, instead of the surveyors being appointed by the parish, they were to be chosen by the justices from a list prepared annually by the vestry. From 1662 a highway rate could be levied to meet the cost of repairs which could not be dealt with by statute labour.

Under the Act of 1691 the highway rate, the levy of which had previously been temporary, was made permanent, but even during the eighteenth century the great majority of parishes, especially those in rural areas, levied no highway rates at all and depended solely on statute labour. It was not until the beginning of the nineteenth century that the highway rate became the normal method of defraying the cost of road maintenance.

Turnpike trusts

Until about the middle of the eighteenth century the main users of the roads in each parish were the local inhabitants, the amount of through-traffic being comparatively small. The development of wheeled traffic, however, especially the introduction of the stagecoach, drew attention to the unsuitability of the parish as a highway authority. The parish was responsible for the repair and maintenance of the highways in its area, but as it was not empowered to build new roads, from the beginning of the eighteenth century it was found necessary to create *ad hoc* authorities for this purpose. These new *ad hoc* authorities, which were set up by local Acts of Parliament, were the turnpike trusts, to which reference has already been made in Chapter 1. Turnpike trusts consisted usually of a number of persons named in the Act as trustees, possessing a definite property qualification. They served for life and filled vacancies by co-option. The trustees were empowered to construct and maintain a specified length of road and to defray their expenses by levying tolls on certain kinds of traffic. By 1835 there were as many as 1100 of these trusts.

The turnpike trustees were extremely unpopular. Throughout the eighteenth century there was rioting in various parts of the country against the inequitable incidence of the tolls, and severe penalties were imposed for the destruction of turnpike gates and houses. As a general rule, the trustees did not employ their own toll collectors, but resorted to the plan of 'farming' or leasing each gate to the highest bidder, who would employ professional 'pikemen' to collect the tolls. There was no central control of turnpike trusts, and their accounts were not required to be audited. Despite all their shortcomings, however, they met a need which the parochial system could not have met and they succeeded in effecting a considerable improvement in the highway system.

From about 1830 the trusts began to feel competition from the railways, and this competition became more and more serious with the rapid development of the railway system. A large proportion of the tolls received by the trusts was collected from stagecoaches, and as railway travel was cheaper and quicker than travel by stagecoach the revenue of the trusts fell, with the result that the trusts gradually came to an end as the term of years expired for which each trust had been established.

Macadam and Telford

From about 1750 onwards the larger and more progressive trusts began to employ salaried officials, but it was not until the beginning of the nineteenth century that surveyors with any technical knowledge were employed. In 1815 John Loudon Macadam (1756–1836), the famous Scottish road-builder and engineer, became surveyor to the Bristol trust, and later consulting surveyor to a number of other trusts. Macadam's policy was to discontinue the use of clay or dirt in road construction and substitute small angular stones for the larger round stones which at that time formed the basis of road surfaces.

Thomas Telford (1757–1834), a Scotsman, who was not only a great road-builder but also a builder of bridges and churches, was engaged to improve the road from London to Holyhead. In 1815 a body of ten Commissioners was set up by the Government for the London–Holyhead road, and Telford worked under their direction. As the turnpike trustees along this stretch of road were not superseded, it was necessary for Telford to persuade each trust to adopt his recommendations.

The Highways Act, 1835

At the beginning of the nineteenth century large stretches of main road were controlled by turnpike trusts, and in rural areas the remaining roads were repaired by the parish. In the majority of urban areas *ad hoc* local authorities known as police commissioners, paving commissioners, street commissioners or improvement commissioners (see Chapter 1) were responsible for the paving, lighting and cleansing of the streets. The need for a more efficient parochial organisation, the competition from the railways (which sounded the death-knell of the turnpike trusts) and the prevailing desire for institutions of a more representative character paved the way for the reform of highway administration.

The Highways Act, 1835, abolished statute labour and repealed nearly all previous enactments relating to road maintenance. The Act retained the parish as highway authority and empowered the vestry, which consisted of the parish ratepayers, to appoint a surveyor, who might be a salaried official. Parishes with a population exceeding 5000 were authorised to elect a representative board of management. Under the provisions of the Act parishes were enabled to combine voluntarily for the purpose of employing a salaried surveyor, but very few parishes availed themselves of this facility.

The need for larger administrative units

Only a large area could afford to employ a salaried surveyor with the necessary technical qualifications, and by gradual stages the area of highway administration was enlarged in the interests of efficiency and economy. The Public Health Act, 1848, made the local boards of health (see Chapter 10) responsible for roads in the newly created urban areas, and the Highways Act, 1862, enabled the justices in Quarter Sessions compulsorily to combine parishes into highway districts. In each highway district the repair and maintenance of roads were entrusted to a highway board, consisting of representatives elected by the constituent parishes and of the local justices, who were ex-officio members. The process of enlarging the area of highway administration was continued by the Local Government Act, 1888, which transferred to the newly created county councils the responsibility for maintaining and repairing the main roads in the county (outside the county boroughs), and by the Local Government Act, 1894, which abolished the highway boards and highway parishes and transferred their functions to the rural district councils. By the end of the nineteenth century, therefore, the confused welter of highway authorities had been considerably simplified. The county council was responsible for main roads, and highways other than main roads were maintained by the councils of boroughs, urban districts and rural districts. In county boroughs all highways were maintained by the county borough council.

In course of time the rapid development of motor traffic made further changes necessary. The Local Government Act, 1929, transferred the highway functions of the rural district councils to the county councils. The need for dealing with through transport travelling along the main traffic arteries led to the passing of the Trunk Roads Acts, 1936 and 1946, under which the Ministry of Transport (now the Department of the Environment) assumed financial responsibility for the most important roads in the country, known as trunk roads. Under these Acts the Department need not carry out the work of maintenance itself but may delegate its powers to the local authority who would otherwise have been responsible for the highway in question.

The present highway authorities

Important changes were made in the Highways Act, 1959, and the Local Government Act, 1972, and the authorities now responsible for the maintenance of highways may be conveniently tabulated as follows:

Authority	*Responsibility*
Department of the Environment	All trunk roads, but the Secretary of State may delegate his functions to local authorities (county or district councils), the Department defraying the cost.
County councils	All other roads.
District councils	They may at their option (subject to reimbursement of expenses from the county council) maintain any highway in their area which is a footpath, bridleway or an urban road other than a trunk or classified road. (Urban roads are main roads with a speed limit of 30 or 40 miles per hour and streets in urban areas. Classified roads are roads and streets of any importance to traffic.)
	Under the Local Government Act, 1972, agency powers for maintenance of highways may be claimed, but if the county council resists the claim, the final decision rests with the Department of the Environment.
Parish and community councils	They may at their option (subject to reimbursement of expenses) maintain bridleways and footpaths.

Great London Council	Metropolitan roads—i.e. those of arterial importance except trunk roads.
London borough councils and City of London Corporation	All other roads.

The central authority

In 1872 the Local Government Board superseded the Home Office as the central authority for highways, and in 1919, when the Local Government Board came to an end, the general supervision of highways became the responsibility of the newly created Ministry of Transport.

The Minister used to classify for purposes of grant all the highways which were of any importance to traffic, but since the passing of the Local Government Act, 1966, Government grants in aid of local authority expenditure on highways are paid as part of the rate support grant.[1] In addition, grants are paid by the Department of the Environment, which is now the central authority for transport services, towards the expenses of highway authorities for the construction of or major improvements to principal roads—i.e. the most important of the classified roads.

Street lighting

Under the Public Health Act, 1875, urban authorities were empowered to light streets, and these powers are now exercised by all district councils. In London the local authorities are the Greater London Council for metropolitan roads and the London borough councils and the City of London Corporation for other roads.

The Local Government Act, 1966, distinguishes between the lighting of roads and footways. Road lighting is the

[1] See Chapter 18.

responsibility of the highway authorities—i.e. the county councils (for trunk roads the Secretary of State for the Environment)—but highway authorities may agree to delegate their functions to the district councils or to the parish or community councils. These authorities are responsible for the lighting of footways.

Street naming and the numbering of houses

Under the Public Health Acts the naming of streets and the numbering of houses were the responsibility of the councils of county boroughs, boroughs, and urban and rural districts. Under the Local Government Act, 1972, these powers are now exercisable by district councils. In inner London, the Greater London Council names and numbers streets, but in outer London the borough councils submit proposals for naming and numbering for the GLC's approval.

Supervision over streets

Under the Highways Act, 1959, and the Local Government Act, 1972, local authorities—i.e. county councils and London borough councils—may make bylaws relating to the level, width and construction of new streets. Local highway authorities may also provide bus and tram shelters, refuse bins, seats, drinking fountains, refuges, subways and guard-rails, and development along roads which are intended to be used for through-traffic can be prevented. Local highways authorities are empowered to require the owner of a tree overhanging a highway to lop or cut the tree, and if the owner fails to comply the authority may carry out the work and recover the cost incurred. The authority is not confined to the supervision of existing streets: land may be acquired by agreement or compulsorily for the improvement of existing highways or the construction of new highways.

Where a private street is made up by the local authority, the cost is charged to the owners of the land fronting on the street. When the works have been completed by the authority, they may take over the street, in which case it will be a public road repairable at the expense of the local authority.

Bridges

Under the Statute of Bridges, 1530, the county or borough in which a bridge was situated was made liable for its repair, and Quarter Sessions was empowered to levy a rate for that purpose. The Local Government Act, 1888, made county councils responsible for most of the public bridges in the county area, and similar responsibilities were imposed on county borough councils. Bridges in trunk roads are the responsibility of the Department of the Environment, but the functions of the Department may be delegated to the local highway authority. Most of the other bridges are now maintained by county councils.

River authorities

Before the operation of the River Boards Act, 1948, catchment boards and drainage boards administered the law relating to the drainage of land, fishery boards dealt with freshwater fisheries and various authorities were empowered to deal with the prevention of river pollution. The purpose of the River Boards Act, 1948, was to concentrate in a limited number of new authorities the related functions of land drainage, flood prevention, fisheries and the prevention of river pollution. The Act empowered the Minister of Health and the Minister of Agriculture and Fisheries to set up river boards, and these boards were established for convenient areas which did not generally coincide with local government boundaries.

The members of a river board were appointed by the two

Ministers concerned and by the councils of the counties and county boroughs whose areas were included wholly or in part in the river-board area. The income of river boards was obtained from various sources, including contributions from the councils of the counties and county boroughs mentioned above.

The Water Resources Act, 1963, created twenty-seven new river authorities, which were made responsible for all water resources, including conservation, land drainage, prevention of pollution and fisheries. Some of the members of these authorities were appointed by local authorities and the remainder by the Minister of Agriculture, Fisheries and Food to represent land drainage, fisheries and agricultural interests, and the Secretary of State for the Environment to represent public water supply and industrial interests.

The Water Act, 1973,[1] established nine regional water authorities and a Welsh National Water Development Authority. These authorities have taken over the functions of the river authorities and responsibility for sewerage, sewage disposal and the supply of water.

[1] See Chapters 10 and 14.

16 Miscellaneous Powers and Duties

This chapter contains an account of the functions of local authorities which do not come within the scope of the preceding chapters.

Small holdings and allotments

For the purpose of affording to persons with agricultural experience an opportunity of becoming farmers on their own account, every county council is required to provide small holdings if there is a demand. Land may be acquired by the local authority (with the approval of the Ministry of Agriculture, Fisheries and Food) by agreement or by compulsory purchase.

Under the Allotments Acts it was the duty of the council of a county borough, borough, urban district or parish to provide allotments if there was sufficient demand for them. For this purpose land could be purchased by agreement or compulsorily, or hired. Now, under the Local Government Act, 1972, parish councils and meetings in England are allotment authorities, but where there is no parish council or meeting the authority is the district council. In Wales allotments are the concurrent responsibility of district and community councils. In London the appropriate authorities are the London borough councils.

The issue of licences

There are certain trades and activities of a varied nature which require either the grant of a licence by a local authority or merely notification to the authority, in which case no licence is issued, and the notification is usually referred to as a registration. The purpose of a licence or registration is to enable the local authority to regulate the conduct of the trade or activity in question (or sometimes the collection of revenue), in accordance with the provisions of the appropriate Act of Parliament. The local authority's powers in relation to licensing are not necessarily greater than those which require registration.

County councils and county borough councils were required to issue licences for drivers under the Road Traffic Act, 1960, and in respect of motor vehicles under the Vehicles (Excise) Act, 1962. The Vehicle and Driving Licences Act, 1969, and the Vehicles (Excise) Act, 1971, however, provide for these functions to be transferred in due course to the Department of the Environment, but in the meantime county and district councils and the Greater London Council may be authorised to act as agents for the Government, to whom the proceeds of these taxes (less the cost of collection) are paid.

Under the Petroleum (Consolidation) Act, 1928, premises where petroleum was stored had to be licensed by county borough, borough or district councils. The present position under the Local Government Act, 1972, is that the licensing authority is the county council, and for London the appropriate authority is the Greater London Council.

Under the Local Government Act, 1972, the authorities now responsible for collecting the fees and issuing local taxation licences—e.g. for dogs, pawnbrokers and money-lenders—are the district councils and the Greater London Council.

Local authorities are also concerned with the issue of licences for public entertainments. Under the Theatres Act,

1968, which abolished the Lord Chamberlain's jurisdiction, theatres were licensed by county councils and county borough councils, and in London by the Greater London Council. The Local Government Act, 1972, substituted the district councils for the county councils and county borough councils outside London. There is a right of appeal to a magistrates' court against refusal of a licence or the imposition of conditions. Under the Cinematograph Act, 1909, and the Local Government Act, 1972, the licensing of cinema performances is the responsibility of the same local authorities, but a licence is usually granted on condition that the film has been approved by the British Board of Film Censors (an unofficial body supported by the trade). If a licence is refused, there is a right of appeal to the Crown Court. There is no longer a requirement of a contribution to charity from the takings of Sunday cinema performances.

Examples of registration by local authorities are the registration of premises where children are looked after by child minders for reward, and the registration of private nursing homes.

Shops and offices

The local authorities dealing with the administration of the Offices, Shops and Railway Premises Act, 1963, were county borough councils, borough councils and district councils. The Local Government Act, 1972, transferred these functions of enforcement to district councils, and in London the responsible local authorities are the London borough councils and the City of London Corporation. The legislation makes general provision for health, safety and welfare, including cleanliness, overcrowding, ventilation, lighting and means of escape in case of fire.

Weights and measures

Under the Weights and Measures Act, 1963, the local authorities for the enforcement of the law relating to weights and measures were the councils of counties and county boroughs and of non-county boroughs and urban districts with a population of at least 60 000. These authorities appointed inspectors whose task was to test weights and measures and to take legal proceedings against offenders. Local administration is now in the hands of county councils, but in Wales a district council may be designated as a local weights and measures authority by order of the Secretary of State. In London the appropriate authorities are the London borough councils and the City of London Corporation.

Consumer protection

In recent years increasing interest and concern have been shown by the Government in the protection of the consumer against unfair trading practices and excessive charges, and the importance attached to this subject has been shown by the appointment by the Government of a Secretary of State for Prices and Consumer Protection and of a Director General of Fair Trading, who, in certain circumstances, may take legal proceedings.

Under the Trade Descriptions Act, 1968, it is an offence for a person in the course of trade or business to apply a false trade description to any goods offered or supplied, or to give false or misleading indications as to the prices of goods. The duty of enforcement devolves on the weights and measures authority, and the inspectorate is becoming increasingly involved in fair trading standards and consumer protection. As a result of the passing of this Act, there has, for example, been a marked improvement in the standards of honesty in travel brochures, a number of offenders having been prosecuted by local authorities. Additional powers were given to the Government and to local weights and measures authorities by the Fair Trading Act, 1973.

Under the Local Government Act, 1972, local authorities

(i.e. county councils and London borough councils) may set up consumer advice centres, and a number of local authorities have, in fact, established such centres based on their weights and measures department. They are intended to provide a comprehensive service to consumers, including pre-shopping advice and facilities for investigating civil and criminal complaints.

Bylaws

Local authorities are primarily administrative (not legislative) bodies, but in making bylaws they exercise a subordinate legislative function.

The Local Government Act, 1933, provided that county councils, county borough councils and borough councils might make bylaws for 'good rule and government', and various other statutes enabled bylaws to be made for specific purposes. Thus, under the Public Libraries and Museums Act, 1964, local authorities may make bylaws regulating the use of libraries and museums, and under the Civil Aviation Act, 1968, local authorities may make bylaws regulating the use and operation of aerodromes which they own or manage. The Public Health Act, 1936, enables local authorities to make bylaws for the regulation of public bathing, and under the same Act bylaws may be made regulating the conduct of persons using public sanitary conveniences.

The provisions in the Local Government Act, 1933, relating to the procedure for making bylaws have been re-enacted with some amendments and simplification in the Local Government Act, 1972. This Act enables district councils and London borough councils to make bylaws not only for the good rule and government of their area but also for the prevention and suppression of nuisances. Other local authorities are still empowered to make bylaws under numerous statutes, covering a wide variety of subjects.

Bylaws must be made under the common seal of the local

authority, and before becoming operative must be confirmed by the appropriate Government department. One month's notice of intention to apply for confirmation must be given in the local press. During this period arrangements must be made for a copy of the proposed bylaw to be deposited for public inspection at the offices of the local authority. When the bylaw has been confirmed, a copy must be available for inspection without payment, and copies must be available for purchase at a sum not exceeding 20p per copy.

For the purpose of securing the greatest possible uniformity throughout the country, Government departments have adopted the practice of issuing model bylaws for the guidance of local authorities, and in general the confirming authority refuses to confirm a bylaw which differs materially from the model bylaw, unless local circumstances justify a departure from the model.

In order to be valid a bylaw must satisfy four requirements. It must be:

1 Reasonable.
2 Within the statutory power of the local authority—i.e. not *ultra vires*.
3 Not repugnant to the general law—i.e. it may only supplement the ordinary law.
4 Free from vagueness and ambiguity.

A bylaw may be challenged, and unless it answers all these tests it may be declared invalid by the court, in which case it would be unenforceable

Bylaws may contain provisions for imposing on offenders reasonable fines, recoverable on summary conviction, not exceeding the sum fixed by the enactment which confers the power to make the bylaw. If no sum is fixed, the maximum fine is £20 and, in the case of a continuing offence, £5 for each day during which the offence continues after conviction.

17 Finance

1 The rating system

The income required by local authorities to administer the services described in the preceding chapters is obtained from four sources: (i) local rates, (ii) Government grants, (iii) trading services and miscellaneous sources (including rents paid by tenants of council houses), and (iv) loans raised by local authorities to meet capital expenditure.

History

The right of local authorities to raise their own local revenues in the form of rates is founded on legislation passed in the Middle Ages and on the Poor Relief Act, 1601. The Act of 1601 empowered the churchwardens and overseers of each parish to assess the rateable value of each hereditament—i.e. each piece of immovable property—and to impose a local tax on the occupier of each hereditament for the purpose of defraying the cost of the relief of the poor of the parish. At first the proceeds of rates were limited to meeting the cost of relieving the poor, but as the functions of local authorities increased, particularly during the nineteenth century, when numerous *ad hoc* local authorities were established, it was found necessary to apply the income from the poor rate to other local government services and to levy new rates, most of which were based on the poor rate assessments.

The Rating and Valuation Act, 1925, abolished the office of overseer and substituted the general rate for the poor rate and other rates which had previously been levied. The parish was replaced as the unit for rating purposes by the county borough, borough, and urban and rural district, these councils being known as rating authorities. The object of this Act was to simplify the assessment and collection of rates and to achieve uniformity of assessment throughout the country.

The basis of assessment

Rates are still levied normally on immovable property, and the rateable value of a hereditament—i.e. the value on which the occupier is assessed for rating purposes—is intended to be the net annual value. The rateable value of dwelling-houses is reached in two stages. First, it is necessary to determine the 'gross value', which is defined as the rent which the tenant might reasonably be expected to pay from year to year if the landlord paid the cost of repairs and insurance, and the tenant paid tenant's rates and taxes. The rateable value is then obtained by deducting the cost of repairs and insurance from the gross value. It is, however, unnecessary to estimate the cost of repairs and insurance, as standard deductions for these expenses are laid down by statute. The application of these principles is designed to ensure that a rateable property, whether it is a dwelling-house or any other structure, is assessed for rating purposes at its market value, as far as it can be ascertained. The law relating not only to the assessment but also to the levying and collecting of rates is now contained mainly in the General Rate Act, 1967.

Exemptions

Under the General Rate Act, 1967, agricultural land and buildings are exempt from rates, and normally no rates are payable by a farmer except for his dwelling-house.

But although the Rating Act, 1971, defined agricultural buildings so as to include buildings which are on agricultural land and are used for keeping or breeding livestock, some agricultural buildings are still rateable. Crown property— e.g. Royal palaces and parks, premises occupied for military purposes and law courts—is exempt from rates, but contributions in lieu of rates are paid by the Treasury to the local authority concerned. Other properties which are exempt from rates include places set aside for religious worship; lighthouses, buoys and beacons; and houses occupied by ambassadors and their staffs. Charities are entitled to 50% relief, and rating authorities have power to reduce or remit the balance. There are special provisions dealing with the assessment of properties occupied by the nationalised industries.

Empty property

For many years all empty property was exempt from rating, but the Local Government Act, 1966, empowered rating authorities to levy rates at half the normal amount on empty property which had been unoccupied for more than three months (six months in the case of new dwellings). The adoption of these powers by local authorities was, however, discretionary, and in most areas empty property was still not rated.

More recently, the question of the rating of empty property received serious consideration by the Government as a result of a number of large office buildings, especially in London, remaining unoccupied for several years. It was alleged that these premises were deliberately kept vacant by their owners to achieve the full financial benefits arising from rapidly increasing office rents and capital values. The efforts of the Government to deal with this problem and with vacant residential property at a time of acute housing shortage culminated in the passing of the Local Government Act, 1974, which provides for rate charges on unused properties up to 100%. In the case of commercial properties the charges are mandatory, and there is a surcharge of double the normal rates in the first twelve months of non-use, rising annually.

The machinery for assessment

The Rating and Valuation Act, 1925, contained a number of provisions for achieving uniformity of assessment. The Act established the principle of quinquennial valuation[1]— i.e. the preparation of a new valuation list every five years —and provided for the setting up of an assessment committee in each area to hear objections to and to confirm the draft valuation list prepared by the rating authority. Moreover, in each county a county valuation committee was assigned the task of securing uniformity within the county, and a Central Valuation Committee endeavoured to fulfil the same purpose for the whole country. Despite all these elaborate safeguards, however, there were wide disparities in the assessment of similar properties in different areas. With the passing of the Local Government Act, 1948, which provided for Government grants to be paid to local authorities on the basis of rateable value, it was particularly important to set up machinery to facilitate uniformity of valuation throughout the country. This Act, therefore, abolished the assessment committees, the county valuation committees and the Central Valuation Committee, and transferred the duties of the rating authority in relation to the valuation of property for rating purposes to district valuation officers of the Board of Inland Revenue.

The work of valuation having been centralised, the valuation officer is now responsible for the preparation of the draft valuation list. The list, which is kept by each rating authority, shows the rateable value of every hereditament in the area. One of the functions of the valuation officer is to consider objections to the draft list. He also deals with

[1] There have, in fact, been only four revaluations during the past fifty years.

proposals to alter the current list, which may be made by
any person aggrieved—e.g. the rating authority or the
occupiers of the premises. Appeals against decisions made
by the valuation officer lie to a local valuation court. This
court consists of the chairman or deputy chairman and two
other members of a local valuation panel set up under a
scheme prepared by the county council and approved by
the Secretary of State for the Environment. There is a right
of appeal against a decision of the local valuation court to
the Lands Tribunal, a body which was established under
the Lands Tribunal Act, 1949. On a point of law a case
may proceed to the Court of Appeal and the House of
Lords.

The making and collection of the rate

The rating authorities are now the district councils and, in
London, the London borough councils and the City of
London Corporation. The financial year runs from 1 April
to 31 March, and the general rate, as it is called, is normally
made for a period of a year. If the rate is levied for a year
it is the usual practice of the rating authority to charge
the rate in two equal instalments—i.e. for the period 1
April to 30 September and from 1 October to 31 March.
The rating authority fixes the rate merely by passing a
resolution. Notice must be given that the rate has been
made, and this is done by fixing notices in conspicuous
places or by publication in the local press. The amount in
the £ at which the rate is to be levied is fixed by the rating
authority, after taking into account its estimated expenditure
and its income from sources other than rates. Let us suppose
that the rateable value—i.e. the total of the assessments of
all the rateable properties in the area—amounts to £10
million and that, after taking into account its estimated
income from other sources during the financial year, the
rating authority finds that a sum of £6 000 000 has to be
raised from rates to meet its obligations. As 10 million times
60p will produce the sum of £6 000 000, the rating auth-

ority will levy a rate of 60p in the £. In the example quoted above, if a house has a rateable value of £200, the occupier will be required to pay £120 a year in rates, i.e. 200 times 60p. This is, perhaps, an oversimplification of the position as a concession is made to domestic ratepayers —i.e. occupiers of residential property—who now pay rates at a lower poundage than other ratepayers. In 1974–5 domestic relief amounted to 13p in the £ for England and 33·5p for Wales. The request for rates is made in the form of a demand note, and if the rate is charged in two equal half-yearly instalments, the first demand will be for the sum of £60 and the second demand will be made six months later for a similar amount. If the ratepayer pays his rates at monthly intervals the monthly payment would be one-twelfth of £120, i.e. £10. The rating demand note must contain certain essential particulars—e.g. the rateable value of the property, the amount in the £ at which the rate is levied, the period in respect of which the rate is made and the amount in the £ levied for each service.

Not every local authority is, however, a rating authority. County councils, the Greater London Council and parish councils, for example, are not rating authorities, and some machinery is necessary to enable these authorities to meet that part of their expenditure which is financed from rates. Authorities which have no rating powers are called 'precepting authorities', as these authorities issue a precept or demand on the rating authority, stating the amount of money they require. The amount required by the precepting authority is not demanded in the form of a lump sum but of an amount in the £ of rateable value. To revert to the example quoted above, the rate of 60p in the £ might be levied by a district council, and as the district council is the rating authority the county council and the parish councils in the area of the district issue precepts on the district council to meet their net expenditure. The rate of 60p in the £, for example, might be made up as follows:

T–I

Rate expenditure of district council	15p
Rate expenditure of county council (met by precept)	43p
Rate expenditure of parish council (met by precept)	2p
Total	60p

The county council, of course, issues a precept not merely to one rating authority but to all the rating authorities included in the area of the administrative county—i.e. to all the district councils—but the parish council issues a precept only to the district council in whose area the parish is situated. The expenditure to be met by a parish council out of rates is comparatively small. Some parishes do not find it necessary to issue a precept, and the amount in the £ of a parish precept varies from one parish to another in the same district. County councils and parish councils are not the only precepting authorities. There may be other precepting authorities, such as parish meetings, joint boards and combined police authorities. In Wales not only the county councils but also the community councils are precepting authorities, and in London precepts are issued on the London boroughs by the Greater London Council and by the Receiver for the Metropolitan Police.

The actual collection of the rate is the responsibility of the rating authority, who may give a discount to occupiers who do not pay their rates by instalments and who make their payments before dates specified by the rating authority. The remedy of a rating authority for non-payment of rates is to apply to a magistrates' court for the issue of a summons. If, after the summons has been served and the occupier has been given an opportunity of appearing before the court, the rate still remains unpaid, the authority may apply to the court for the issue of a distress warrant, which authorises the rating authority to seize the furniture and goods of the defaulting ratepayer and sell them. If the proceeds of sale are insufficient to satisfy the warrant, the defaulter may be committed to prison, but a committal warrant may not be issued by the court except in cases of

services (with the exception of trading services and the personal health services) administered by local authorities has been steadily expanding, and this growth of responsibility has led to an increase in expenditure, with the result that local government has been compelled to rely to an increasing extent on Government grants.

From 1835, when the first Government grant was made (towards the cost of criminal prosecutions), for more than half a century, grants in aid of local expenditure were mainly on a percentage basis. These payments to local authorities, which included grants in aid of police, poor relief, vaccination, highways and the maintenance of pauper lunatics, were largely replaced in 1888 by a system of 'assigned revenues'. Under this scheme of financial reorganisation the proceeds of certain taxes, which were considered to be of an expanding nature, were assigned by the Government to local authorities, the intention being that the assigned revenues would keep pace with the increasing expenditure of the local authorities. This hope, however, was not fulfilled, and between 1888 and 1929 the Government found it necessary to pay to local authorities fresh grants for specific services. The system of assigned revenues was finally abolished by the Local Government Act, 1929, which made important changes in the financial relationship between the central government and local authorities.

The Local Government Act, 1929
A number of grants for specific purposes were discontinued, and these were replaced by a block grant to each county and county borough on a formula basis, calculated by reference to the population of the area, weighted by the following factors:

1 The number of children under the age of 5.
2 Low rateable value.
3 Abnormal unemployment.
4 Sparsity of population.

The block grant also included compensation to local authorities for loss of rates by derating. The grants were paid by the Government direct to county councils and county borough councils, and each county council redistributed a portion of the grant to the boroughs and urban and rural districts in the county on the basis of flat population. To avoid too much disturbance to local government, arrangements were made for these financial provisions to operate by gradual stages over a period of seventeen years, and grants for a number of services—e.g. for police, education, roads and housing—were left outside the block grant.

Exchequer equalisation grants

The transfer of hospitals from local authorities to the Ministry of Health under the National Health Service Act, 1946, and the transfer of public assistance services from local authorities to the National Assistance Board by the National Assistance Act, 1948, necessitated a complete revision of the financial relationship between the Government and local authorities. The block grant introduced by the Local Government Act, 1929, was replaced by the Exchequer equalisation grant, which was based, like the former block grant, on weighted population but calculated on a formula which was designed to ensure that the poorer local authorities obtained a larger measure of assistance. The weighted population was calculated by adding to the actual population the number of children under 15, so that they counted twice, and in the case of county councils there was an additional weighting for sparsity of population. The rateable value of the whole country was then divided by the weighted population of all the counties and county boroughs, and in this way the average rateable value per head of weighted population was obtained. If in any county or county borough the rateable value per head of weighted population fell short of the national average, the local authority was credited by the Exchequer with the deficiency in rateable value, and rates were paid by the Government to each county and county borough on the credited rateable value. This represented the amount of the Exchequer equalisation grant. Some counties and county boroughs received no Exchequer equalisation grant, as their rateable value per head of weighted population was above the national average. Except in the County of London, where special arrangements were made, whether a county council received an equalisation grant or not it was required to pay to each county district in its area a capitation grant. The Minister of Housing and Local Government was empowered to reduce the grant if he was satisfied that a local authority had failed to achieve or maintain a reasonable standard of efficiency and progress in the discharge of its functions or that the expenditure of the local authority had been excessive or unreasonable. The grants paid by the Exchequer towards the cost of administering specific services, e.g. education, housing, police and highways, were not abolished, and the total amount of these grants was considerably greater than the amount of the Exchequer equalisation grant.

The Local Government Act, 1958

In July, 1957, the Government issued a White Paper on Local Government Finance in England and Wales. At the time of the publication of this document about seven-eighths of all Exchequer grants were given in the form of specific grants. The White Paper proposed that in future only about one-third of all Exchequer assistance should be given in the form of specific grants and that the remainder should be distributed to local authorities in the form of a general grant in aid of their expenditure. The substance of these proposals was embodied in the Local Government Act, 1958.

The general grant (frequently referred to as 'the block grant') took the place of many of the specific grants (most of which were percentage grants) payable by the Government to county councils and county borough councils. This grant absorbed the Exchequer grants for health, education, the care of children and the aged, grants for the fire services, and a number of smaller grants, but not the grants payable for housing, highways and the police. It was distributed to local authorities in accordance with a complicated formula, which was intended to ensure that areas with the greatest financial needs would derive the maximum benefit. Included in the factors which were taken into account in assessing the grant for each authority were the population of the area, the number of children under 15, the proportion of children at local schools and the number of infants and old people. Provision was made in the Act to reduce general grants in cases where local authorities had failed to maintain reasonable standards.

The Exchequer equalisation grants, which were payable to local authorities under the Local Government Act, 1948, continued to be paid, but they were renamed rate deficiency grants. These rate deficiency grants were payable, however, not only to county councils and county borough councils but also to the councils of those county districts and metropolitan boroughs whose rateable resources were below the national average.

The Local Government Acts 1966 and 1974

Important changes in Government grants were made by the Local Government Act, 1966, which introduced the rate support grant. This grant consists of three elements: the needs element, the resources element and the domestic element.

The needs element (by far the largest of the three elements) replaced the general grant, and its distribution— now only to non-metropolitan county councils, metropolitan district councils and London borough councils, in view of their heavy expenditure on education and social services— is based on the population of the area weighted by several factors, including the number of children under the age of 15 and under the age of 5, the number of people over the age of 65, high or low density, declining trend of population, education, personal social services and high-ways expenditure, and high costs in the Metropolitan Police District. The resources element, which is the former rate deficiency grant in a new form, is payable to those county councils, district councils and London borough councils with a substandard rateable value per head of population, which for 1974–5 has been calculated by the Government at £154. The domestic element provides rate relief to domestic ratepayers—i.e. to the occupiers of dwelling-houses and flats. Rating authorities reduce the rate poundages on domestic properties by a sum fixed by the Secretary of State for the Environment, which for 1974–5 is at the rate of 13p in the £. There is a smaller reduction for mixed properties—i.e. properties which are used partly as dwellings and partly for other purposes. The loss of revenue to the authority is made up by the domestic ele-ment in the rate support grant. In London 40% of the rate support grant payable to the inner London boroughs is paid over to the Greater London Council to be applied towards the expenditure incurred by the Inner London Education Authority.

The total rate support grant payable to all local auth-orities for 1974–5 is at the rate of 60·5% of relevant expendi-ture, which is expected to amount to £5273 million. The rate support grant is well in excess of the yield from rates. The grant may be reduced if the Minister considers that the services provided by an individual authority have fallen below prescribed standards. There are still a number of specific grants payable to local authorities, including grants for police (50%), for housing (under the Housing Finance Act, 1972), for town and country planning, the construction or major improvement of principal roads and the administra-tion of justice. These and a number of new grants introduced under the Local Government Act, 1974, are deducted from the rate support grant total. The new grants relate to rate rebates (90%), awards to students for first degree university

courses and comparable courses (90%), and grants for
teacher training (90%), transportation and national parks.
The transportation grant, which will start in 1975–6,
covers expenditure on public transport, highways, regulation of traffic and the provision of car parks.

Special provision for the needs of immigrants

The Local Government Act, 1966, empowered the Home
Secretary to make grants to local authorities who had to
make provision for a substantial number of immigrants.
Under the Local Government Grants (Social Needs) Act,
1969, a specific grant (in addition to the rate support grant)
is payable by the Government to a limited number of local
authorities of special social need. Finance has been made
available at the rate of 75% of expenditure for 'urban
aid programmes' covering a wide variety of experimental
projects in the field of health, nursery education, child care,
etc.

3 Loans

The justification for borrowing by local authorities

Local authorities are under no legal necessity to borrow,
but in practice all but the smallest local authorities find it
expedient to raise money by loan. In managing their
financial affairs, private individuals do not normally resort
to permanent large-scale borrowing, and it may well be
asked why local authorities do not regulate their finances
in such a way as to render borrowing unnecessary. In other
words, why cannot local authorities balance their expenditure against their current income without raising loans?

In the first place, if there were no loan expenditure by
local authorities, rates would fluctuate violently from one
year to another. As wide fluctuations in rate poundages are
most inconvenient and undesirable, it would be far more
prudent for the local authority to raise the money required
by loan, and in that way to spread the cost of expensive

projects over a number of years. Loan expenditure by local authorities can further be justified on the ground that as such expenditure is of a reproductive nature, involving the creation of tangible assets, posterity shares in the benefits and should help to pay for them. By comparison with national standards, borrowing by local authorities is not excessive: the loan debt of local authorities in England and Wales is now approaching £20 000 million, compared with a National Debt of about £35 000 million. Local authority debt, however, is now increasing at a very rapid rate, and the cost of servicing loans—i.e. payment of the interest and the repayment of the capital plus management expenses— represents a substantial proportion of the budgets of the majority of local authorities.

The policy of Parliament has been, and still is, to allow local authorities to borrow but to insist on financial safeguards. Local authorities are not permitted to incur permanent debt: they must provide for redemption of their loans within a certain number of years. They are, therefore, in a different position from limited companies, who may raise loan capital without any obligation to make provision for repayment. Normally loans are allowed only for permanent works, and there is the additional safeguard that a major loan requires the approval of the Secretary of State for the Environment, who fixes the period of repayment— e.g. sixty years. Under the Local Government Act, 1972, however, local authorities are empowered to borrow money temporarily to defray expenses pending the receipt of revenue without obtaining loan sanction, and, in addition, the consent of the Secretary of State is not required for loan transactions of a minor character. In 1970 a distinction was drawn between 'key-sector' schemes, which continued to require specific approval, and 'locally determined' schemes, which local authorities were free to undertake within an overall annual limit of expenditure. Key-sector schemes include housing, education, police, principal roads, and personal health and social services. Locally determined schemes include fire services, libraries, parks, baths, refuse collection and disposal, and the administration of justice. Early in 1974 the Secretary of State, in an effort to contain inflation, decided to withhold loan sanctions for some key-sector expenditure and reduced allocations for the locally determined sector.

Methods of borrowing

The purposes for which local authorities may borrow are set out in the Local Government Act, 1972, and in other statutes which empower local authorities to borrow for specific purposes.

Many local authorities obtain most of their loan requirements from the Public Works Loan Board, a statutory body which was originally established to lend money to the smaller local authorities who might otherwise have experienced difficulty in raising money at a low rate of interest. The amount which local authorities may borrow from the Board is limited. For authorities in the less prosperous areas the loan quota is higher than that allowed to other authorities. The rate of interest charged to local authorities by the Public Works Loan Board is fixed by the Treasury. In recent years owing to mounting inflation, the rates of interest on money borrowed by local authorities have reached unprecedented levels; in 1973 interest rates as high as 16% per annum were paid on some short-term local authority loans, and since then have been even higher rates of interest payable for long-term loans. In an effort to obtain loans at a lower rate, local authorities sought powers to borrow on the foreign money-market. In 1970 more than fifty of the private Bills promoted by local authorities contained powers for the authority to borrow money abroad. The Local Government Act, 1972, enables local authorities to borrow money outside the United Kingdom or in a foreign currency, but only with the consent of the Treasury. Early in 1974 the Greater London Council negotiated the largest loan ever obtained by a local authority: 500 million

eurodollars (approximately £215 million) were borrowed
from a syndicate of international banks.

Local authorities may raise money by means of mortgages secured on the whole of their revenues, and they may
borrow by the issue of local authority bonds. Many local
authorities have advertised in the local and national press
fixed-term loans at market rates for periods of six months
to five years, which are of interest to the small investor. The
Chartered Institute of Public Finance and Accountancy
has a loans bureau with offices in London which operates
on a non-profit-making basis and provides investors with
up-to-date information about all types of local authority
loans, ranging from overnight money to longer term mortgages on bonds. Local authorities also borrow by utilising
internal funds—e.g. employees' superannuation funds.

4 Audit

The necessity for audit

Since local authorities, in carrying out their powers and
duties, spend large sums of public money, it is necessary to
ensure as far as possible that extravagant or illegal expenditure is avoided and that the interests of the ratepayer and
the taxpayer are protected. In order to achieve this object
it is essential for the accounts of local authorities to be
audited. It may be argued that as local authorities, in the
main, are representative assemblies, any audit of their
accounts, especially by an officer of the central government,
is an unwarrantable interference with democratic local
government. But the mere fact that local authorities are
popularly elected bodies does not necessarily ensure that
the funds with which they are entrusted will be spent with
due care and for purposes authorised by law, and some
further safeguard is therefore necessary.

The origin of audit

The Poor Relief Act, 1601, provided that the churchwardens

and overseers should submit their accounts annually to the local justice of the peace for approval. Although the checking of accounts by the justices, who usually had little or no knowledge of finance, was largely ineffective, occasionally items of expenditure were disallowed, and the officers concerned were required by the justices to repay the money to their successors in office. The Poor Law Amendment Act, 1834, despite the fact that it introduced a large measure of central control, allowed each board of guardians to appoint its own auditor, but in 1868 the appointment of auditors was transferred to the Government, and as new local authorities were brought into existence provision was made for their accounts to be audited by auditors who were centrally appointed. This form of audit, however, did not apply to the accounts of municipal corporations. They remained subject to the amateur system of audit introduced by the Municipal Corporations Act, 1835. Of the three borough auditors, two were known as 'elective auditors'. These two auditors, who were elected annually (usually on 1 March) by the local government electors, could not be members or officers of the council, and they were not required to have professional qualifications or experience, but they had to be qualified for election as councillors. A third auditor was appointed by the mayor from amongst the members of the council, and in his case, too, there was no requirement as to professional qualifications or experience. These three auditors had no power of surcharge,[1] and they conducted an audit which was often described as archaic. Under the Local Government Act, 1933, however, a county borough or non-county borough was empowered by resolution passed by a two-thirds majority to adopt either the system of district (Government) audit or professional audit. Professional auditors had no power of surcharge, but they had to be members of a recognised professional body of accountants. A number of municipal corporations availed

[1] See p. 226 below.

themselves of this power to adopt district or professional audit.

The District Auditors Act, 1879, reorganised the system of audit on a national basis, and the District Auditors, as they were called, became civil servants, who later audited the accounts not only of the boards of guardians but also of the new local authorities (except county boroughs) which were established under the Local Governments Acts, 1888 and 1894. For the purpose of checking the accounts of local authorities, which were made up to 31 March, a District Auditor was appointed by the Government department concerned (now the Department of the Environment) for each district into which the country was divided for audit purposes. Until the coming into operation of the Local Government Act, 1972, the position was that the accounts of the Greater London Council, London borough councils, parish councils and parish meetings, and urban and rural district councils were audited by the District Auditor. Some municipal corporations—i.e. some county boroughs and non-county boroughs—had adopted district or professional audit. In the remaining boroughs and county boroughs some of the accounts—e.g. those relating to education, health, rating and the social services—were subject to district audit, but the other accounts were audited by borough or professional auditors.

The present system of audit

The Local Government Act, 1972, which made important changes in the arrangements for audit, requires all accounts of local authorities to be made up yearly to 31 March or such other date as the Secretary of State for the Environment may direct, and every local authority must make arrangements for the proper administration of its financial affairs. All the accounts of every local authority must be audited either by a District Auditor or by an approved auditor—i.e. a professionally qualified auditor, whose appointment requires the approval of the Secretary of State.

The choice lay with the local authority, and it had to be exercised by 1 January 1974. Provision is made in the Act for the local authority, with the approval of the Secretary of State, to change its mind at a later date. London authorities are at present subject to district audit but may choose between District Auditors and approved auditors from 1 April 1976.

District audit procedure

The District Auditor notifies the local authority whose accounts are to be audited of the date of the audit, and arrangements are made for the relevant documents to be deposited at the office of the local authority for a prescribed period before the audit. During this period any local government elector may inspect the documents and take copies of them, and at the audit he may raise objection to any item in the accounts.

Before the coming into operation of the Local Government Act, 1972, if, in the course of scrutinising the accounts, the District Auditor found that a payment had been made which was contrary to law, he had to disallow the item and surcharge the person responsible. In other words, it was his duty to require the member or officer who authorised or incurred the expenditure to repay the amount to the local authority. Under the Local Government Act, 1933, a person who was aggrieved by a surcharge, or who objected to an item of expenditure and was not satisfied with the Auditor's decision, had a right of appeal. If the amount exceeded £500 the appeal lay only to the High Court, but in other cases the appeal could be made either to the High Court or to the Secretary of State for the Environment, and the Court or the Secretary of State could confirm, vary or quash the decision of the Auditor. The Act further provided that a person surcharged, whether or not he appealed, could apply to the High Court or the Secretary of State for a declaration that he acted reasonably or in the belief that his action was authorised by law. He could then, at the discretion of the

Court or the Secretary of State, be relieved, wholly or in part, from personal liability in respect of the surcharge.

The Local Government Act, 1972, has simplified the system without making substantial changes in its effect. Although the powers of disallowance and surcharge have been abolished, if a person fails to bring into account a sum which ought to have been included, or where there is a deficiency due to wilful misconduct, the District Auditor may certify that the amount due is recoverable by the authority concerned from the person responsible. There is a right of appeal to the High Court (or, where the amount does not exceed £750, to either the High Court or the County Court) by an aggrieved party who is named in the certificate or by a local government elector who has appeared at the audit and has made an unsuccessful objection. If the sum involved exceeds £2000 and the appeal fails, the person liable, if he is a member, is disqualified from membership for a period of five years. Furthermore, if the District Auditor considers that an item in the accounts is contrary to law he may apply to the Court for a declaration to that effect, in which case the member or officer responsible may have to refund the amount to the local authority out of his private resources, and if the amount exceeds £2000 the member may be disqualified from membership of a local authority for a specified period.

Any expenditure which has been sanctioned by the Secretary of State cannot be the subject of the issue of a certificate or an application for a declaration, but such expenditure may nevertheless be challenged in the courts by an interested person.

The extent to which an auditor could control extravagance by a local authority is illustrated by the case of *Roberts* v. *Hopwood*. In 1921–2 the Poplar Borough Council, which was empowered to pay its employees such wages as it deemed fit, paid a minimum wage of £4 a week to its male and female workers. The District Auditor drew attention to the fact that these wages were considerably in excess of those paid for similar work by other local authorities and by other employers in the same locality, but as the local authority, wishing to be regarded as a model employer, persisted in its policy, the District Auditor surcharged the members of the council with the sum of £5000. The Auditor's decision was upheld by the House of Lords on the ground that the wages paid by the council were so excessive as to be contrary to law.

A more recent case involving the District Auditor, which aroused acrimonious political passions, was that of the eleven councillors of Clay Cross (Derbyshire) Urban District Council, who refused to implement the provisions of the Housing Act, 1972, relating to increases in rents of council tenants amounting to £1 a week. The councillors lost their appeal to the Divisional Court against the District Auditor's surcharge of £6985 and were ordered to pay his costs of £2000. They were also disqualified from membership of the council for a period of five years.

The approved auditor
The powers and duties of an approved auditor differ, to some extent, from those of a District Auditor. Local government electors have no right to appear at the audit, and an approved auditor cannot certify that an amount is due to a local authority from a person responsible or apply to the Court for a declaration that an item of expenditure is contrary to law. In such circumstances, however, he is required to report the matter to the Secretary of State, who may then decide to hold an extraordinary audit by a District Auditor. An extraordinary audit may also be requested by a local government elector who wishes to question an item in the accounts audited by an approved auditor.

18   Central Control

The nature of central control and its justification

Central control over the activities of local authorities is exercised in three forms: by Parliament, by the Government departments and by the courts. The control of local authorities by Parliament is legislative, by Government departments mainly administrative and by the courts judicial. Reference has already been made (in Chapter 7) to the supremacy of Parliament in relation to the services which local authorities are empowered to provide, and it remains to deal in this chapter with the supervisory functions of Government departments and the courts of law.

There can be little doubt that some measure of departmental control is necessary. Despite the fact that local authorities are democratically elected assemblies and that the large authorities employ salaried experts who are competent to advise them on technical matters, it would be unwise to give local authorities unfettered discretion in the management of their own affairs. Whereas local authorities obtain their information and experience from a limited field, the knowledge acquired by the officials of Government departments in dealing with problems arising over a wide area is necessarily more extensive and varied in its scope. Furthermore, central control enables the Government to put into operation a policy which individual local authorities may find irksome or unduly restrictive of their initiative but which is nevertheless justified by considerations of national interest. Finally, Government departments can and do lay down minimum standards of administration below which the services of local authorities are not allowed to fall.

There is equal justification for judicial control. There should be some machinery to ensure that an individual who suffers from arbitrary or inconsiderate treatment on the part of a local authority is provided with a judicial remedy if other forms of redress are not available. Judicial remedies may also enable Government departments to deal with refractory local authorities in cases where administrative action is inappropriate or inconvenient.

The development of central administrative control

Until the early part of the nineteenth century the justice of the peace, who was the chief functionary in local government, was allowed to discharge his varied administrative duties unhampered by central direction. But the Poor Law Amendment Act, 1834, which was largely inspired by Jeremy Bentham, an ardent advocate of Government supervision, introduced a considerable measure of central control over the newly established boards of guardians. The Act set up the Poor Law Commissioners, a central body which was empowered to issue orders relating to the management of the poor and the formation of parishes into unions, and to appoint inspectors and dismiss local officers without the consent of the board of guardians. The Municipal Corporations Act, 1835, however, which reformed the boroughs, provided for little central control over these authorities. Central control had been imposed on poor law guardians with some reluctance and mainly with the object of reducing expenditure on poor relief. The only important function entrusted to the reformed corporations was the management of the police, and it was not foreseen at the time that these corporations would be required to administer other local government services. It was felt, therefore, that rigid supervision by a central authority was unnecessary. The autonomy granted to municipal corporations in 1835, however, is no longer enjoyed by them.

The central authority responsible for the administration of the poor law continued to exercise close and detailed supervision over the local authorities until the final abolition of the poor law by the National Assistance Act, 1948. The Board of Guardians (Default) Act, 1926, went so far as to empower the Minister of Health, in certain circumstances, to replace the members of a board of guardians by the Minister's own nominees. Control by Government departments over local authorities in relation to other services was not so pronounced, but services such as education and police, which received substantial Government grants, were, and still are, subject to a considerable measure of central direction.

The principal central departments concerned with the control of local authorities are now the Department of the Environment, the Department of Education and Science, the Department of Health and Social Security, and the Home Office. Central departments with supervisory functions in relation to local government also include the Ministry of Agriculture, Fisheries and Food, the Department of Prices and Consumer Protection, and the Treasury. The most extensive measure of control over local authorities is exercised by the Secretary of State for the Environment, who is a member of the Cabinet and is assisted by four Ministers responsible for special aspects of the work (most of which relates to local government) of this huge department and by two junior Ministers, who are Undersecretaries of State. The four Ministers concerned are the Minister for Planning and Local Government, the Minister for Housing and Construction, the Minister of State (Urban Affairs) and the Minister of State (Sport).

There is a Secretary of State for Wales, who has a seat in the Cabinet, and he is assisted by a Minister of State. The

Welsh Office, which is centred in Cardiff, is responsible for matters relating generally to local government in Wales and for primary and secondary education, housing, town and country planning, highways and certain health services.

Methods of administrative control

Reference has already been made to the part played by Government departments in controlling the activities of local authorities by auditing their accounts, giving grants in aid of their expenditure, and approving their loans and their bylaws. These Government departments also have certain powers relating to the appointment and dismissal of some local officials and to the fixing of their qualifications. These powers are dealt with in Chapter 19. Other methods of departmental control are dealt with below:

(a) Informal control

Circulars and letters containing advice or giving instructions to local authorities are from time to time sent by Government departments, especially when new legislation is passed or new regulations are issued. Consultations are held between the officials of the local authority and those of the central department, and problems which arise are sometimes dealt with by semi-official correspondence of an informal character.

(b) Inspection and inquiries

Many Acts of Parliament make provision for inspection by officers of central departments of services administered by local authorities. Thus, Home Office inspectors inspect police services and fire services, community homes are inspected by the Department of Health and Social Security, and the Department of Education and Science has inspectors for schools and colleges. The inspector reports on the efficiency of the service, and his report is submitted to the appropriate department for such action as is considered necessary. Inspectors give the officers of the local authority guidance and advice in carrying out their duties. Under various statutes they may hold public local inquiries and preside at informal hearings—e.g. in a dispute between the local authority and a private individual, or in cases where the local authority has asked for approval of a loan—and the inspector reports his findings to the Minister or department concerned.

(c) Control of building

In order to ensure that local authorities build schools, houses, etc. with due regard to the limited supply of skilled labour and materials available and to the needs of the national economy, and that buildings comply with official requirements, capital projects may not be undertaken without the approval of the appropriate Government department. Such approval involves the submission of plans and estimates by the local authority. Government departments exercise a measure of control over certain local authority expenditure by imposing cost limits and yardsticks on the construction of buildings, such as primary and secondary schools, community homes and homes for the aged.

(d) Approval of schemes

Many important Acts of Parliament have required local authorities to submit schemes to Government departments for approval, showing in detail how the services to be undertaken will be organised. This practice was followed, for example, in the Education Act, 1944, and the Housing Finance Act, 1972, provides that rent rebate and rent allowance schemes made by local authorities are subject to any directions which may be issued by the Secretary of State for the Environment.

(e) Default powers

Most of the statutes dealing with local government contain provisions which enable the appropriate Minister or department to deal with a recalcitrant local authority. Thus, under the Public Health Act, 1936, if a local authority has failed to discharge its statutory functions, the Department of the Environment may make a default order requiring the authority to comply with the terms of the order within a stipulated time, and this order may be enforced by court proceedings. As an alternative, the Secretary of State may, if the defaulting authority is a district council, make a further order transferring the functions to the county council. The Housing Finance Act, 1972, went so far as to empower the Secretary of State as a last resort not only to make a default order but also to appoint a Housing Commissioner to exercise the functions of the defaulting local authority and to charge it with the expenses incurred by him. A member of a local authority who wilfully obstructs a Housing Commissioner is liable on summary conviction to a fine of up to £400. Several local authorities, including Clay Cross Urban District Council (Derbyshire), who resolutely opposed the Act on political grounds, acted in defiance of the law relating to increases in rents for council tenants, and in a few areas Housing Commissioners were, in fact, appointed by the Government to enforce the law.

(f) Delegated legislation

The tendency of modern Acts of Parliament is to lay down broad principles of policy in the statute itself and to leave the details to be filled in later in the form of orders, rules or regulations made by the appropriate Minister. The comprehensive term applied to these orders, rules and regulations is 'statutory instruments'. Parliament, in effect, delegates a part of its legislative power to Government departments by enabling them to make statutory instruments, which have the force of law. The validity of these statutory instruments, however, may be challenged in the courts on the ground that they are *ultra vires*—e.g. because in making the regulation in question the Minister has exceeded the powers conferred on him by the Act or because the prescribed procedure has not been followed. The procedure for making statutory instruments was standardised by the Statutory Instruments Act, 1946. Some of the most important statutory instruments require an affirmative resolution of Parliament before they come into operation, whilst other instruments are subject to annulment by a resolution of either House within forty days.

Statutory instruments are far more numerous than Acts of Parliament and are used extensively by Government departments in issuing directions to local authorities. Thus, under the Police Act, 1964, the Home Secretary is empowered to make regulations for the government, pay, clothing and conditions of service of the members of all police forces; and under the Clean Air Acts, 1956 to 1968, which are administered by local authorities, the Secretary of State for the Environment may make regulations prescribing limits on the rates of emission of grit and dust from chimneys and furnaces.

(g) Quasi-judicial powers

A large number of statutes confer upon Government departments the power to adjudicate in disputes, including cases involving local authorities. The Education Act, 1944, for example, empowers the Secretary of State for Education and Science to determine a dispute between a local education authority and the governors or managers of a voluntary school; under the Local Government Act, 1972, agency powers for the maintenance of highways may be claimed by a district council, but if the county council resists the claim the final decision rests with the Department of the Environment; and under the Town and Country Planning Act, 1971, if a person is refused permission by the local planning authority to develop land, he has a right of appeal to the Secretary of State for the Environment. In these respects administrative bodies, despite the fact that they are entrusted with functions of a judicial chracter, need not follow the ordinary rules of procedure of a court of law.

Increases and relaxations in central control

Successive governments, both Labour and Conservative, have paid lip-service to the value of local democracy, and responsible Ministers have from time to time declared their firm intention to release local authorities from some of the irritating controls to which they are subjected and from some of the financial fetters, which limit their powers of discretion. Despite these fervent utterances by politicians, the policies adopted in recent years have followed no consistent pattern. During the 1960s, for example, Government departments exerted administrative pressure on local education authorities in securing the adoption of a policy of comprehensive education throughout the country, and local authorities were precluded by the Government from selling more than a tiny fraction each year of their homes to council tenants. Detailed controls continued to be added to the statute book. Thus, the Public Libraries and Museums Act, 1964, empowered the Minister to fix the level of library fines for overdue books. In 1969–70, as part of their national policy of retrenchment, the Labour Government insisted that collectively the expenditure of local authorities should not, in real terms, exceed by more than 3% the amount spent in the previous year, and even more stringent controls over revenue and capital expenditure of local authorities were imposed by the Conservative Government at the beginning of 1974. The Housing Finance Act, 1972, virtually removed from local authorities the power to determine the rents payable by council tenants. These directives have been resented by many local authorities, who feel that they are a serious encroachment on their freedom of action and an unwarrantable interference with local democratically elected bodies in the management of their own affairs.

There has, however, in recent years also been some measure of relaxation of central controls. During the period of office of the last Conservative Government (1970–4) local authorities were free to determine whether or not they should adopt a policy of comprehensive education; and restrictions on the sale of council houses were removed. In 1971 local authorities were given freedom to undertake 'locally determined' schemes within an overall annual total of expenditure without the necessity of obtaining express loan sanction from the central authority. Furthermore, the opportunity was taken in the Local Government Act, 1972, to remove a number of restrictions—e.g. in relation to the appointment of statutory officers and committees—and the Local Government Act, 1974, relaxed or removed controls in a large number of minor matters. Although local authorities are subject to a substantial measure of central direction, they are not merely the agents of Whitehall, and considerable scope is left for the exercise of local initiative and discretion over a wide field of public service.

Judicial control

In this country (unlike many other countries) local authorities and their officers are subject to the same courts and the same legal system as are private individuals. A private individual, for example, can sue his local council and, if he is successful, obtain damages from the council in satisfaction of his claim.

Judicial control of local authorities is not limited to the right of an aggrieved individual to sue a local authority for damages. There are, in addition, remedies available to secure the performance by local authorities of their statutory duties or to restrain them from acting outside their jurisdiction. One of the most important of these remedies is the order of *mandamus*, which is an order granted by the High Court commanding any person, corporation or inferior court to carry out a public duty. Thus, in 1922, the Poplar Borough Council, which had refused to pay the LCC precept, was compelled to do so by *mandamus*. A further example of *mandamus* is contained in the Education

Act, 1944, which provides that if a local education authority fails to discharge a duty the Secretary of State for Education and Science may make an order against the local education authority, and if the terms of this order are not complied with the Department may apply to the High Court for a *mandamus*. This remedy applies only to the performance of an absolute duty (not a discretionary power), and the procedure is not available if any other remedy is equally convenient. The effect of non-compliance with an order of *mandamus* is that the members of the offending authority may be imprisoned for contempt of court.

If a local authority is contemplating the commission of an act outside its jurisdiction—e.g. making a payment which is contrary to law—the local authority may be prevented from doing so by an injunction, which is issued by the High Court. A private individual who wishes to obtain an injunction against a local authority, however, must join the Attorney General as nominal plaintiff unless some private right of his own is infringed. Private individuals and the Attorney General may also bring an action for a declaration. In an action of this kind the plaintiff merely asks the Court for an authoritative statement of his rights. Although a declaration does not provide the means of enforcement, it is a useful remedy in cases where the law is obscure.

Lastly, excess of jurisdiction may, in certain circumstances, be dealt with by an order of prohibition or by an order of *certiorari*, issued by the High Court. An order of prohibition prohibits an inferior court from continuing proceedings in excess of its jurisdiction, and *certiorari* deals with the same kind of case, except that it is used where the proceedings of the court have already been completed. Orders of prohibition and *certiorari* have been obtained to control not only inferior courts in the strict sense but also Government departments and other public bodies (including local authorities) when making judicial decisions in the course of carrying out their administrative duties. Thus, an order of prohibition or *certiorari* might be obtained if a local authority, in exercising a power to issue a licence for a public entertainment, failed to act in a judicial manner in reaching its decision, and *certiorari* has been used to quash a valuation list made by a valuation officer.

19 Local Government Officers

The development of a salaried local government service

Until the beginning of the nineteenth century the administration of local government was not, as a general rule,
entrusted to salaried officers. The justices of the peace,
despite the fact that they occupied a pivotal position in
county and parochial government, were unpaid; the parish
officers—the churchwardens, overseers, surveyors of highways and constables—received little or no remuneration
for their public services; the turnpike trustees, who 'farmed'
their toll-gates to the highest bidder, had little need for the
employment of paid officials; and the unreformed municipal corporations, who were concerned chiefly with the
management of corporate property, rarely found it necessary to appoint a salaried officer.

As the services administered by local authorities increased in scope and complexity, the need for the employment of salaried officers became more evident. From about
the beginning of the nineteenth century it was not unusual
for the office of county treasurer to become a salaried
appointment. At about the same time, turnpike trustees
began to employ salaried surveyors, and in some of the more
populous parishes, which could no longer rely on unpaid
amateurs to shoulder the growing burden of parish administration, regular salaries were paid to vestry clerks,

assistant overseers and workhouse masters. The Metropolitan Police Act, 1829, and the Municipal Corporations Act, 1835, provided for the appointment of paid police officers; the Poor Law Amendment Act, 1834, enabled boards of guardians to employ salaried officers on a large scale; and the General Highways Act, 1835, allowed parish vestries and highway districts to appoint salaried surveyors. By 1835 the long-established practice of employing unpaid officers had definitely been abandoned in favour of whole-time salaried appointments.

The local government service today

Despite the fact that many important services have been transferred from local authorities to the state and to national corporations, there are about two and a half million persons employed by about 450 separate authorities in local government today. These include staff in administrative, professional, technical, clerical and miscellaneous grades, and manual workers. Membership of trade unions is encouraged by some local authorities, and a high proportion of local government officers are trade union members. The National and Local Government Officers' Association (NALGO) has about 530 000 members, but many of these are employed in public services outside local government. Other local government employees are members of the General and Municipal Workers' Union, the National Union of Public Employees, and the Transport and General Workers' Union, or of professional unions—e.g. the National Union of Teachers—or craft unions for such trades as building and engineering.

In serving a local authority, an employee is making a direct contribution to the public welfare. Although expectations of advancement are often not as high as those in the world of industry and commerce, and monetary rewards are not spectacular, the local government service is a 'sheltered occupation' which offers an employee an interesting and progressive career, giving reasonable security of tenure not only during periods of prosperity but also in times of trade recession. This does not imply that an employee has a legal right to be retained in the service of a local authority so long as he is efficient and his conduct is above reproach. In practice, however, a local authority rarely dispenses with the services of an employee who satisfies these conditions, despite the fact that under the Local Government Act, 1972, an officer holds office on such reasonable terms and conditions as the appointing authority thinks fit.

Another attraction of service in local government is the advantage enjoyed by full-time officers and the majority of manual workers of participating in a superannuation scheme. Local government superannuation schemes, which are made under the Local Government (Superannuation) Acts, 1937 to 1972, are contributory. An officer, for example, may be required to contribute 6% of his salary throughout the whole of his service, and the employing authority contributes an equal or greater sum, but provision is now made for voluntary retirement at the age of 60 after the completion of 25 years' service. The maximum age of retirement is normally 65. An officer employed by one local authority who obtains an appointment with another local authority carries with him his superannuation rights, and similar provision is made in cases where an officer of a local authority secures a post in the service of a public authority outside the sphere of local government. There are separate superannuation schemes relating to special classes of local government employees—e.g. for teachers and for employers of the Greater London Council—and for the police.

The origin of Whitleyism

During the First World War a committee was set up by the Government under the chairmanship of Mr J. H.

Whitley, Speaker of the House of Commons, to devise means of settling industrial disputes by negotiation. In accordance with the recommendations of this committee, 'Whitley Councils' were set up by the Government in a number of industries and also for the Civil Service. Efforts to adapt this machinery to local government, though at first unsuccessful, culminated in 1944 in the establishment of a reconstituted National Joint Council for Local Authorities' Administrative, Professional, Technical and Clerical Services. This body now consists of members appointed by the employing authorities and by the staff side. In 1946 the National Joint Council succeeded in reaching agreement on a national scheme of salaries and conditions of service for administrative, professional, technical and clerical staff employed by local authorities.

The National Joint Council mentioned above is not concerned with all the local government employees whose remuneration and conditions of service are regulated by Whitley machinery. There are many other bodies constituted on similar lines which are responsible for special classes of local government employees. Thus, there is the National Joint Council for Local Authorities' Services (Manual Workers), which has continued to function since its inception in 1919; there are joint negotiating committees for chief executives of local authorities and their chief officers; there is the Police Council; the National Joint Council for Local Authorities' Fire Brigades; and the Burnham Committees (for teaching staff). These bodies are so numerous and their decisions gave rise to so many complex questions that in 1948 it was found necessary for employing authorities to set up a co-ordinating body known as the Local Authorities' Conditions of Service Advisory Board. This body provides an advisory service for local authorities. The great majority of local authorities have accepted the decision of these national bodies without question, but where it is claimed that recognised terms or conditions of employment which have been settled by

representative organisations of employers and employees
have not been observed, the claim may be referred to the
Department of Employment. If the Secretary of State is
unable to settle the claim he must refer it to the Industrial
Arbitration Board (a body which was formerly named the
Industrial Court). An award of this Board is enforceable in
the courts.

The 'Charter'

The agreement concluded in 1946 by the National Joint
Council dealt with the salaries and service conditions of
administrative, professional, clerical, technical and miscellaneous staff employed by local authorities in receipt of
salaries of not more than £700 a year, but there is now no
'ceiling'. The salaries and conditions of service of staff
covered by this agreement and its amendments were popularly referred to as the 'Charter'. The staff concerned are
classified in three divisions, and the National Joint Council
in its publications has given information relating to the duties
and responsibilities of officers employed in each division.

The three main divisions are now: the Clerical Division,
the Administrative and Professional Division (the A.P.
Division) and the Technicians and Technical Staffs Division. The Clerical Division, which has three grades, covers
posts with duties of a clerical nature, and in the higher
grades includes supervisory posts. Promotion to posts in
clerical grades 2 and 3 is on merit, but local authorities
are required to give preference to staff who have passed the
Clerical examination. The last Clerical examination, however, was held in December, 1973, and clerical staff are
now encouraged to prepare for the Certificate in Office
Studies and the Ordinary National Certificate in Public
Administration. The Administrative and Professional
Division, which has five grades (grades 1, 2, 3, 4 and 5
upwards in order of seniority) consists of officers who are
professionally qualified—e.g. solicitors, architects, engineers

and surveyors—or who are in a responsible capacity concerned with the general administration of the authority's
work or the improvement of its organisation. Above AP
grade 5, there are grades for Senior Officers and Principal
Officers. The positions in these grades are sometimes filled
by officers who are not only qualified by examination but
are also widely experienced in administrative or professional work. The Technicians and Technical Staffs Division,
which has five grades (grades 1, 2, 3, 4 and 5 upwards
in order of seniority), consists of staff who undertake work
of a technical nature requiring special training or expertise.
This division includes draughtsmen, clerks of works, building
inspectors and laboratory technicians. There are also special
classes of officers—e.g. librarians, education welfare
officers, home teachers of the blind, shorthand-typists and
machine operators—for whom there are separate scales.

The adoption of a national standard

Before the adoption of a national standard of salaries and
service conditions, the remuneration of local government
officers performing similar duties varied considerably from
one locality to another. The operation of a national standard, however, is intended to ensure equal pay for equal
work throughout the country. The grading of an employee
is left in the first instance to the individual local authority,
but some progress towards a reasonable measure of uniformity of grading has been achieved by an appeals
procedure, which enables an employee who is dissatisfied
with his grading to appeal to a Provincial Council—i.e. a
body composed of staff and employers' representatives
whose functions include the determination of appeals. In
recognition of the higher cost of living in London (particularly expenditure on housing and fares), a London
weighting (which is higher for inner London than for outer
London) is added to the national scales. The inadequacy
of this weighting has resulted in acute shortage of staff in

London, especially for planners, architects, valuers, social workers, public health inspectors and residential home staff. NALGO has pressed very strongly for a substantial increase in London weighting, and in the first half of 1974 militant action was taken by staff in support of their demands, including a series of strikes of their members employed by London boroughs.

Throughout the negotiations with the employers' representatives the staff insisted on equal pay for men and women, but although this principle was not at first conceded except as far as the administrative, professional and technical grades were concerned, equal pay was later granted by graduated stages. The Greater London Council has its own staff gradings and its own negotiating machinery, and male and female staff in the Council's service in all grades have for a long time received equal pay.

Recruitment and training

Before the Second World War local authorities normally recruited their employees at the age of about sixteen, and the general educational standards demanded was the School Certificate, but during the War it was found necessary to relax this standard. In 1953 it was decided to establish a national entrance examination, the intention being to attract to a career in local government pupils not only from secondary grammar schools but also from secondary modern schools. This national examination consisted of three papers—English, arithmetic and general knowledge. It was conducted by a national body, known as the Local Government Examinations Board, which was established by the National Joint Council. The national entrance examination was, however, largely ignored and was later discontinued. Candidates are now accepted in the Clerical Division if they have passed the General Certificate of Education Examination at Ordinary Level or the Certificate of Secondary Education (CSE), but owing to the lack of suitable candidates some local authorities have found it necessary to accept applicants without either of these qualifications.

The NJC Scheme of Conditions of Service provides for the recruitment of local government officers from the widest possible field, including persons holding university degrees. University graduates are recruited direct and are normally appointed to the Administrative and Professional Trainee Grade. Unfortunately, however, to university graduates and undergraduates a career in local government presents a rather dull and unglamorous image with limited horizons, and, apart from the service of the Greater London Council, the proportion of university graduates recruited to administrative posts is comparatively small. Facilities are offered to staff who enter as juniors, and sometimes to more mature staff, to study for university degrees in their spare time. Many local authorities, especially the larger local authorities, have organised schemes of post-entry training for their junior officers, not only to assist them in studying for degrees, professional qualifications and local government promotion examinations but also for the purpose of enabling their staff to take a wider and more intelligent interest in their daily duties. Some local authorities allow their employees to attend courses of instruction at polytechnics, technical colleges or colleges of commerce for one day a week or on a block-release basis—e.g. for six or eight weeks' continuous full-time training—in the council's time. Courses are also arranged for local authorities by joint action through the agency of Provincial Education Committees and by the Local Government Training Board, which was formed in 1967 and, in the following year, took over the duties of the Local Government Examinations Board. The Board imposes a voluntary levy on local authorities on a manpower basis, and the main proceeds of this levy are repaid to local authorities who undertake training courses for their staff. Courses of an advanced nature for chief officers and their deputies are arranged by the

Institute of Local Government Studies at Birmingham University. There are graduate courses in local government, and the post-graduate degree of MA in local government is awarded by the University of Kent at Canterbury. The NJC Scheme emphasises the importance of continued study for officers after entry to the service, and makes provision for the payment of all prescribed course fees and other approved educational expenses arising from the attendance of officers at courses of instruction.

The majority of the qualified professional staff employed by local authorities are recruited to the service after they have obtained their professional qualifications, but some local authorities encourage and provide facilities for their unqualified staff to obtain their qualifications whilst they are in the employ of the local authority.

Promotion from one division to another

If an officer wishes to obtain promotion from one division to another he is required to pass a qualifying examination conducted by the Local Government Training Board. An officer who aspires to promotion to the AP Division (in which there are five grades) should either obtain the qualification of a recognised professional body or pass the Administrative examination. The Administrative examination is in two stages—intermediate and final—and the standards are those of the intermediate and final stages conducted by professional bodies. The examination is intended to provide the candidate with a broad mental training as well as to test factual knowledge relating to his administrative duties. Success in the final examination entitles the candidate to the award of the Diploma in Municipal Administration (DMA). The existing examination system is, however, now in the process of change. The last intermediate DMA examination under the old regulations was held in April 1974, and the last final examination will be held in 1976. The new DMA examination is in two stages: a Certificate in Municipal Administration (CMA) at pass degree level, followed by the Diploma in Municipal Administration at the level of the finals of major professional examinations. Candidates for the CMA examination must have five passes in the GCE examination in certain approved subjects, of which two are at advanced level.

Promotion to the AP Division is not automatic on the passing of the appropriate examination: it can take place only if a vacancy exists on the authorised establishment. The Local Government Training Board has approved a number of alternatives to its own examinations. A degree of a British university or the final examination of certain recognised professional bodies, for example, confers eligibility for promotion to any administrative post in the local government service. Despite the NJC recommendations, however, local authorities continue to appoint and promote to the AP Division staff who have shown merit and have the required experience but have neither the DMA nor an alternative qualification.

Conditions of service

The NJC Scheme deals not only with remuneration, qualifications, recruitment, promotion and training but also with conditions of service generally. Such questions as hours of duty, payment for overtime, annual and maternity leave, discipline, payment during sickness and motor-car allowances are prescribed on a national basis. The Scheme also lays down a code of official conduct. Thus, a candidate for appointment must disclose in writing his relationship with a member of the employing authority or with any of its senior officers. Deliberate omission to disclose such a relationship disqualifies a candidate, and if the omission is discovered after the appointment has been made the candidate is liable to dismissal. Canvassing of members of a local authority by a candidate is not permitted, and any attempt to canvass, either directly or indirectly, disqualifies the candidate. The Local Government Act, 1972, requires an officer to disclose any pecuniary interest he may have in a contract which is entered into by his employing authority, and this requirement is dealt with also in the Scheme. In short, the local government officer is expected to give his employers his unswerving loyalty, to maintain a high standard of integrity and not to place himself in a position which might cause a conflict between his private interests and his official duties.

Negotiating committees for chief officers etc.

Collective bargaining in local government does not exclude the most senior officers, for whom there are separate negotiating committees. Salary ranges for chief executives in the new local authorities were agreed by the Joint Negotiating Committee for Clerks of County Councils and the Joint Negotiating Committee for Town Clerks and District Council Clerks (now the Joint Negotiating Committee for Chief Executives). Agreement on chief officers' ranges of pay has been reached by the Joint Negotiating Committee for Chief Officers and by the National Joint Council for Administrative, Professional, Technical and Clerical Services for chief officers within the scope of the NJC. These agreements, instead of laying down a fixed scale, provide for a range of salaries based on the population of the area and also for an appropriate percentage of the salary of a chief officer to be paid to deputy chief officers.

Local freedom in making appointments etc.

With certain exceptions referred to below, a local authority is allowed a free hand in appointing its officers. The Local Government Act, 1933, empowered local authorities to appoint such officers as might be necessary and to pay them such reasonable remuneration as the authority might determine. Some appointments, however, were obligatory. A county council, for example, was required to appoint a clerk, a treasurer, a medical officer, a surveyor, a chief education officer and a director of social services. Under the Local Government Act, 1972, local authorities are now required to appoint such officers as they think necessary for the proper discharge of their functions. Statutory appointments of officers for specified purposes are no longer obligatory, except that non-metropolitan county councils, metropolitan district councils and London borough councils must appoint chief education officers[1] and directors of social services; and county councils must appoint chief fire officers, agricultural analysts, and weights and measures inspectors. In addition, chief constables, deputy chief constables and assistant chief constables must be appointed under the Police Act, 1964. A few local authority appointments still require the approval of a Government department. The appointment of a chief constable, for example, is, under regulations made by the Home Secretary, subject to his consent. The Secretary of State for Social Services may make regulations prescribing the qualifications of directors of social services, and he may veto the appointment of a person whom he considers to be unfit for the post. The Secretary of State for Education and Science may veto the appointment of a chief education officer. As regards salaries, quite apart from the necessity of adhering to national salary scales, there has not been complete freedom because local authorities, in common with other employers, have been required to comply with the provisions of the Counter Inflation Act, 1973, and the directions of the Pay Board.

The chief executive officer and the chief officers

Until recently the clerk was regarded as the council's chief administrative officer, and the great majority of the clerks of the larger local authorities were solicitors. The office of

---

[1] Only outer London boroughs are required to appoint chief education officers. In inner London education is the responsibility of the Inner London Education Authority.

clerk or town clerk of a local authority was in no sense comparable to that of managing director of a business organisation. He was not, as a general rule, empowered to give instructions to the other chief officers, but his duties usually included the co-ordination of all departments of the council in order to avoid overlapping and, as far as possible, to secure procedural uniformity. He was expected (if he was a solicitor or barrister) to advise the council on the legal aspects of its work; to act as secretary to the council by attending its meetings and assuming responsibility for the preparation of the agendas and minutes; and sometimes to conduct all correspondence with Government departments and in matters of policy. In some American and Canadian cities and in a few cities in Eire, a City Manager has been appointed to control the affairs of the city. Usually he has authority to appoint and dismiss all the administrative officers and to act as the executive head of the city, subject to the general control of the council on matters of finance and policy.

The Maud Committee on the Management of Local Government (1967) and the Mallaby Committee on the Staffing of Local Government (1967) both recommended that the clerk should head the authority's service and have authority over the other chief officers. Even before the publication of these two reports a few local authorities had made appointments of 'chief executive officer' or 'town clerk and chief executive officer' with wider powers than those of town clerk, and these officers were selected for their administrative ability and management skills rather than their legal qualifications or experience of local government. Newcastle-upon-Tyne, for example, in 1965, appointed Mr Frank Harris, a former production executive, to the position of 'principal city officer with town clerk'. Since the issue of the Maud and Mallaby reports, many of the larger local authorities have appointed chief executive officers, giving them authority over the other chief officers, except where the professional discretion or judgment of the chief officer is involved or he is exercising responsibilities placed on him by statute.

Additional impetus to the appointment of a chief executive officer or chief executive officer and town clerk rather than a clerk or town clerk has been afforded by the publication in 1972 of the report of the Bains Committee on Local Authority Management Structures and by the operation of the Local Government Act, 1972. The Bains Committee recommended that there should be a corporate approach to local government through a chief executive, who should not carry departmental responsibilities, although the larger authorities might find it necessary for him to have one or two assistants. The Committee proposed that the chief executive should be the leader of the officers' management team and that as head of the council's paid service he should be given authority over all other officers so far as this was necessary for the efficient discharge of the council's functions. The Local Government Act, 1972, facilitated appointments of chief executive officer by dispensing with the necessity of appointing a clerk or town clerk. All chief executives have been invited to join the Society of Local Authority Chief Executives (SOLACE), a professional society for promoting the competence and knowledge of chief executives. Under the Education Act, 1944, many local education authorities gave the title of director of education to their chief education officer, and under the Local Authority Social Services Act, 1970, local authorities responsible for the administration of social services were required to appoint a director of social services. It is now a common practice for local authorities to place each of their departments under a director. Advertisements have appeared in the press, for example, for directors of finance, housing, planning, development, consumer services, leisure activities, environmental services, and recreation and amenities. The terminology of the appointments made by local authorities since the Local Government Act, 1972, came into operation shows that an immense variety of posts has been created, some of which have unfamiliar titles previously unknown to local government. Comparatively few appointments have been made from outside the field of local government, and although some local authorities have appointed their treasurers as chief executive officers (possibly in the belief that an accountant is best qualified to grapple with the complexities of new management techniques) and one London borough appointed a district auditor, the great majority of chief executive officers are solicitors. Most authorities now prefer to employ a chief personnel officer or personnel officer rather than an establishment officer to deal with matters relating to staff.

Management services

The Mallaby Committee on the Staffing of Local Government, which reported in 1967, recommended that local authorities should recognise the need for officers to receive formal training in management and that authorities should make greater use of management services to assist decision making. Management services include corporate planning and management, organisation and methods (O & M), work study, operational research and the use of computers.

The main object of corporate planning is to enable members of local authorities to give purposeful direction to the administrative machine. Corporate planning and management, as envisaged in the Bains Report (1972), involve the preparation of a corporate plan for the local authority extending over a period of several years. Priorities are established and objectives clearly defined, and allocations are made of resources of money, manpower and land to achieve these objectives. Essential features of corporate planning and management are the establishment of a policy and resources committee and the appointment of a chief executive officer as leader of the officers' management team. A successful corporate plan must be adhered to as far as possible, but it cannot be inflexible as it may have to be varied in the light of changed conditions and unforeseen developments.

An O & M officer is a specialist who examines problems of administration and organisation in order to devise the most efficient and economical managerial methods. Many local authorities, instead of employing their own O & M staff, have sought the assistance of outside business consultants. The Greater London Council has its own O & M organisation and the London boroughs have combined to form the London Boroughs Management Services Unit, which was established more than twenty years ago. An increasing number of local authorities are using work-study techniques in relation to manual employment and the promotion of incentive schemes, and local authorities have also shown great interest in operational research, which may be described as the application of scientific methods to the solution of the wide variety of problems encountered in any large-scale public or commercial enterprise. The Local Government Operational Research Unit was established by the Royal Institute of Public Administration in 1965, and its services have been made available to a wide range of authorities, who make payments on the basis of rateable value towards the expenses incurred by the Unit. It has the advantage of being in a position to carry out research on a scale impossible even for the largest local authorities. In 1974, for example, the Unit carried out an investigation on the utilisation of waste products for heating and other purposes, and the study covered an area of 455 square miles of Yorkshire. OR has also been used in determining optimum car-parking space at council offices to meet the demands of council members, staff and visitors.

When computers were first used in local government their use was confined to accounting work, including the calculation of wages, superannuation, income tax and overtime, thus relieving staff of clerical routine work and performing it with greater accuracy. It is now the intention to exploit the computer as far as possible in the service of management so that it can carry out more sophisticated assignments. In one authority, for example, there is a computer which compares the advantages and disadvantages of alternative constructional designs by working out the comparative specifications and costs. In London the GLC, in co-operation with the police, has started to control traffic signals by computer, and it has been estimated that centralised computer control techniques save about 10% of travel time. The Local Authorities Management Services and Computer Committee (LAMSAC), which was established in 1968, conducts research, arranges training courses and disseminates to local authorities information relating to management services and computers.

The place of the specialist in local government

The senior officers of a local authority, especially heads of departments, usually possess professional qualifications appropriate to the duties which they are expected to carry out. The chief executive officer is, as a general rule, a solicitor, the director of finance is an accountant, the director of education is required to have had some experience as a teacher and the director of social services must have relevant qualifications in social studies or social administration. In this respect there is still a marked contrast between the policy of local authorities and that of the Civil Service, but the contrast is not so clearly evident as it was only a few years ago. The chief executive officer of a local authority, even if he is a solicitor, may now be concerned mainly with management functions, and the legal work of a local authority is now often carried out by other qualified officers—e.g. by a deputy town clerk or by a county secretary and solicitor. In the Civil Service, although most of the highest appointments are still normally held by men and women who were recruited in their early and middle twenties direct from the universities and who have no specialised qualifications, as a result of the acceptance by the Government of the report of the Fulton Committee (1968) that the service should develop greater professionalism and that specialists should have wider opportunities for participation in management, the Civil Service practice is undergoing gradual change. Generally speaking, however, it is still true to say that in the Civil Service it is the administrator who takes the decisions after consultation with his expert advisers, whilst in local government decisions of senior staff without reference to the council or its committees are taken by professional officers, and it is the professional officer who, as head of his department, has authority to recommend a course of action to his employing authority. Whereas in the Civil Service, generally speaking, the administrator is on top and the professional adviser is on tap, in local government the position is reversed.

It is arguable whether it would be in the interests of local government to apply the Civil Service practice of appointing to the highest posts men and women who have given proof of administrative ability or management skill. On the one hand, it is contended that if the highest administrative appointments are restricted to candidates with expert knowledge, the field of selection is severely limited; that very few of the hundreds (or perhaps thousands) of decisions which a departmental head is called upon to make in the course of a year call for expert knowledge; and that if professional or technical advice is needed, the expert is always available for consultation. On the other hand, it is argued that a number of cases can be cited of professional officers who have utilised their expert knowledge in achieving outstanding success as administrators, and that the administrator, although he has the expert at his elbow, may, owing to ignorance of the subject-matter of the problem with which he is faced, neglect to seek the advice of the expert when it is necessary to do so. There is little doubt, however, that the Civil Service practice could be applied only to the larger local authorities and those of medium size as, despite the reorganisation of the structure of local government in 1974, the financial resources of the smaller local authorities are still insufficient to permit the employment of more than one senior officer in each department; and if only one such officer is to be employed, it is essential that he should have the necessary specialised knowledge and experience.

20 London

The importance of London and its special problems

London has been aptly described by Carlyle in *Sartor Resartus* as 'that monstrous tuberosity of civilised life, the capital of England'. For more than a hundred years after these words were written, the population of the metropolis continued to expand to an extent which Carlyle or his contemporaries could hardly have envisaged. There has, however, during the past three or four decades, been a continuous decline in the population of Greater London from well over eight and a half million in 1939 to about seven and a quarter million at the present time, and, according to forecasts made by the Greater London Council, the fall in population is likely to continue.

The immense size, wealth and influence of London, and the fact that it is the seat of government, have presented problems of a special nature to the legislature and to the local administrator. Britain contains a number of 'conurbations'—i.e. groups of neighbouring towns which have grown into continuous built-up areas—particularly in the Midlands and Lancashire. None of these conurbations, however, has developed to the mammoth size and importance of London, and such difficulties as have arisen in dealing with their administration are not comparable to those relating to London. In London the firmly entrenched privileges of the City Corporation, the concentration of more than one-seventh of the entire population of England and Wales and about 28% of its rateable value in a comparatively small area, and the great importance of the metropolis as a commercial, industrial, political and administrative centre have all played their part in producing problems requiring separate legislation.

Although the two-tier structure of local government in Greater London does not differ materially from that of a large metropolitan county, local government in London raises problems which in many respects are unique. Whilst the population has been declining since the beginning of the Second World War it has become more cosmopolitan in character, and during this period there has been a phenomenal increase in the number of tourists. To describe London as a Mecca for tourists is no exaggeration. The number of tourists visiting Britain in 1974 is expected to exceed eight million, and there is little doubt that the great majority will spend the whole or most of their time in London. Although tourism is an asset to the country's economy, the influx of tourists involves local authorities in additional problems relating to accommodation, traffic, refuse, etc. From time to time there have been suggestions for the levy of a special tax on tourists from abroad in aid of London rates, having regard to the additional strain imposed on London local government services.

The problem of the homeless, which has already been dealt with in Chapter 11, has assumed greater dimensions in London than in any other city. Many of the London boroughs are under continuous pressure to accommodate an increasing number of homeless people, not only Londoners but people who are attracted by the lure of the capital city, and the problem is aggravated by the fact that in London there is a demand for labour. Residential accommodation in London (whether for purchase or renting) is much more costly than it is elsewhere, and there is a greater scarcity. In recognition of this, and of the cost of travel from the suburbs to the centre of London, local authority staff are paid a London allowance, but until recently this was considered by the staff to be woefully inadequate, and London local authorities experienced great difficulty in recruiting and retaining staff.[1] Another reason for the acute shortage is that staff employed by London local authorities, especially in central London, have to spend much more of their time in travelling to and from their work, often in conditions of extreme discomfort in overcrowded vehicles. It is, perhaps, not surprising that local government officers and manual workers in London boroughs tend to be more militant and more ready to withdraw their labour than those employed elsewhere.

What is London?

The term London is used in so many different senses that it would be well, before attempting to deal with its machinery of government, to arrive at an understanding of what is meant by London. The place occupied by each type of local authority mentioned below in the pattern of London government will be explained later in this chapter.

First, there is the City of London—i.e. the square mile in the heart of the metropolis—which is administered by the City of London Corporation. Although its night population is comparatively small, its day population is estimated at several hundred thousands. The area of the Inner London Education Authority (formerly the approximate area of the London County Council), which contains the City and the twelve inner London boroughs, is about 117 square miles and its population is about 2 700 000. (In 1931 it was 4 000 000.) The area administered by the Greater London Council is 610 square miles and the population is about 7 250 000. The Metropolitan Police District covers about 786 square miles with a population of about 8 000 000. The area served by London Transport

[1] In 1972–3 London boroughs spent £1 000 000 on agency fees for clerical, typing and professional staff.

Executive is 900 square miles. The London postal area covers an area of 253 square miles. The Metropolitan Water Board, which ceased to exist on 1 April 1974 when the Water Act, 1973, came into operation, served an area of 570 square miles. It will be seen from the explanation given above that a clear comprehension of the relationship between the many administrative areas loosely referred to as London is essential to a study of its government.

London government before 1855

London at one time meant the City of London, and until the end of the eighteenth century there was some justification for the claim of the City to regard itself as London, since although the population of the square mile was already decreasing, the wealth, influence and life of London were still largely concentrated within its boundaries. Outside the City there was no local government of London as a whole. There was a welter of some 300 small local bodies (most of which had been established by local Acts), consisting mainly of parish vestries, paving commissioners, lighting commissioners and turnpike trustees with limited functions, discharging their responsibilities with little or no regard to the wishes or interests of the inhabitants whom they were supposed to represent. Corruption was rife, administrative standards were deplorably low and the lack of a unifying authority for the whole of London was conducive to inefficiency, even in those areas where some attempt was made to establish a workable system. The Metropolitan Police Act, 1829, and the Poor Law Amendment Act, 1834, brought about a decided improvement in public security and in the administration of poor relief, but the Municipal Corporations Act, 1835, which reformed the boroughs, did not apply to London, chiefly because of the implacable opposition of the City of London Corporation, which was intent on retaining its traditional independence and ancient privileges. This unsatisfactory state of affairs, which could hardly have been tolerated for an indefinite period, was to a great extent remedied by the Metropolis Management Act, 1855.

The Metropolis Management Act, 1855

The Act defined the boundaries of the Administrative County. In twenty-three of the largest parishes a vestry, elected by the ratepayers, was established and fifty-nine smaller parishes were grouped into fifteen districts administered by district boards. In these smaller parishes the method of election was indirect—the ratepayers of the constituent parishes elected the parish vestry, whose members then elected the members of the district board. The members of the vestries and district boards served for three years, one-third retiring annually. Voting was by show of hands, and five ratepayers could demand a poll. Each vestry or district board was required to appoint a medical officer of health and an inspector of nuisances, and the duties of the vestries and district boards included the paving, lighting, watering and cleansing of the streets, the construction and maintenance of local sewers, the removal of refuse, and the prevention and abatement of nuisances.

The Act of 1855 provided for the establishment of a central body for an area corresponding closely to the Inner London Education Authority known as the Metropolitan Board of Works. It consisted of a chairman and forty-five members, three of whom were elected by the City Corporation, two by each of the six largest vestries, one by each of seventeen other vestries and the remainder by the district boards. The members were elected for three years, one-third retiring annually. The original functions of the Board included the provision and maintenance of main sewers and sewage disposal works, the making and widening of important streets, the regulation of buildings, the naming of streets and the numbering of houses. Later the Board acquired powers in respect of the acquisition and maintenance of parks and open spaces, slum clearance, the construction of tramways, the management of the fire brigade, and the repair and maintenance of the Thames bridges.

The Metropolitan Board of Works was, on the whole, not a success. Perhaps its chief defect lay in the unsatisfactory method by which its members were elected. Election was indirect even in the case of those members of the Board who were elected by the vestries, and even more indirect where the members of the Board of Works were elected by the district boards. Even if the Board had carried out its duties with impeccable efficiency and honesty of purpose it is doubtful whether its work could have commanded much interest or enthusiasm.

The Board of Works suffered, in addition, from other disadvantages. There were too many local authorities in its area exercising functions over which the Board had no control. The boards of guardians established by the Poor Law Amendment Act, 1834, remained untouched; to make matters worse, in 1867 a new authority, known as the Metropolitan Asylums Board,[1] was set up for the area covered by the Metropolitan Board of Works to provide treatment for sufferers from infectious diseases; and in 1870 the London School Board was established as the local authority for elementary education. The Metropolitan Board of Works had no control over these authorities or over the City Corporation, except that within the City boundaries it was responsible for the fire brigade and main drainage. Moreoever, although the Metropolitan Board of Works was empowered to approve the loans of vestries and district boards and to compel these authorities to construct new local sewers, it had no general powers of supervision or coercion.

Nevertheless the Metropolitan Board of Works could claim a great deal of meritorious work. The construction of an efficient main drainage and sewage disposal system;

[1] The Metropolitan Asylums Board continued its existence until 1930, when its functions were transferred to the LCC.

the making or widening of a number of famous streets; the construction of Victoria Embankment and Albert Embankment; and the establishment and maintenance of an efficient municipal fire brigade are achievements for which the Board will be remembered.

The work of the Board came to a rather abrupt and inglorious end. A Royal Commission in 1887 investigated allegations of corruption by officials and members of the Board in the allocation of sites to speculators, and when the Local Government Bill for the establishment of county councils was drafted in 1888 the opportunity was taken to terminate the existence of the Board and to transfer its functions to the newly created London County Council.

The London County Council

On its formation in 1889 the LCC acquired not only the functions of the Metropolitan Board of Works but also certain powers formerly exercised by the justices in Quarter Sessions, including the licensing of theatres and the management of lunatic asylums. The other local authorities in the area of the new county remained unaffected by the establishment of the county council. The Local Government Act, 1888, provided for the election of the county councillors by the ratepayers at three-yearly intervals and for the election of aldermen by the councillors to the number of one-sixth of the number of councillors. Lord Rosebery was the Council's first Chairman.

Party politics have played an important part in London government, and from its inception in 1889 until 1907 the majority party on the LCC were the Progressives, who consisted of Liberals and a few members of the Fabian Society. The advanced political outlook of the County Council was regarded with strong suspicion by Lord Salisbury, who, in the course of a speech made in 1894, referred to the Council's headquarters as 'the place where collectivist and socialistic experiments are tried and where a new revolutionary spirit finds its instruments and collects its arms'. It has been said that when the London Government Act, 1899, replaced the vestries and district boards by the metropolitan boroughs, the boroughs were given an existence largely independent of county council control with the deliberate purpose of checking the aggrandisement of the Progressive County Council.

The constitution of the LCC was similar to that of other county councils, except that in London the aldermen numbered one-sixth (instead of one-third) of the councillors. The County Council consisted of 126 councillors (three for each of the forty-two electoral divisions of the County) and twenty-one aldermen. The Council met at fortnightly intervals.

The powers and duties of the LCC were, on the whole, more extensive than those of other county councils. The County Council was the education authority for the county (there were no 'excepted districts' or divisional executives in London); it was responsible for main drainage over an area much larger than the Administrative County; under the provisions of the London Building Acts it was the authority for regulating the construction of buildings; it maintained 107 parks, some of which were outside the county boundary; it embarked on vast schemes of slum clearance and owned huge housing estates, many of which were outside its area. Broadly speaking, it can be said that, with the exception of police and library services and the maintenance of roads, which in London were not county responsibilities, the functions of the LCC were similar to those of other county councils, with the addition of the functions referred to above.

It is perhaps unfortunate that for the greater part of its existence the Council was of a different political complexion from the Government of the day. Throughout almost the whole of the period from 1889 to 1907 there was a Conservative Government and a Progressive Council. Reference has already been made in this chapter to the friction which arose between the Council and Lord Salisbury, who was Prime Minister from 1886 to 1892 and from 1895 to 1902. In 1934 there was a clash between the Labour Council and the National Government on the rebuilding of Waterloo Bridge. The Council insisted on demolishing the old bridge and building a new bridge in its place, but the Government, being equally determined that the old bridge should be reconditioned, refused to sanction a loan, whereupon the Council decided to defray the cost from the rates. Eventually the dispute was settled amicably and the Government gave a grant in aid of the rebuilding. Another example of a dispute arising from difference of political outlook was provided early in 1954, when the Council's policy of building comprehensive secondary schools received a serious setback as a result of the refusal of the Minister of Education to sanction the closing of a grammar school from which it was intended to transfer pupils to a new comprehensive school. One should not conclude from these incidents, however, that throughout its existence the Council was continuously at loggerheads with the Government. Despite political differences, the relations between the Council and the Government of the day were, on the whole, quite cordial and any disagreements which on occasions arose on matters of policy did not seriously impair the efficiency of London's administration.

The metropolitan borough councils

Like the councils of boroughs outside London, the metropolitan borough councils consisted of a mayor, councillors and aldermen, but whereas in boroughs outside London the proportion of aldermen was one-third of the number of councillors in the metropolitan boroughs the proportion was (like the LCC) one-sixth. A further difference was that in a borough outside London one-third of the members of the council retired each year, but in the metropolitan boroughs all the members of the council retired simultaneously.

The functions of the metropolitan boroughs differed from those of the non-county boroughs outside the metropolis. The metropolitan boroughs, as 'sanitary authorities', were like other boroughs responsible for paving, cleansing and scavenging the streets, and for the removal of refuse, and their functions also included the levying and collection of rates, the administration of the Food and Drugs Act, the preparation of electoral registers and the provision of entertainment under the Local Government Act, 1948. Some services, however, for which non-county boroughs outside London had sole responsibility, were administered partly by the LCC and partly by the metropolitan borough councils. Thus, in London local sewerage was a borough council function, but the LCC was the main drainage authority; the larger London parks were maintained by the County Council and the smaller open spaces by the boroughs; and both the LCC and the metropolitan boroughs were responsible for housing. On the other hand, the metropolitan boroughs were the library authorities to the exclusion of the LCC and were also responsible for the maintenance of all highways, with the exception of trunk roads.

Proposals for the reform of London government

Following a resolution adopted by the LCC, asking the Government to investigate the reform of London government, a Royal Commission under the chairmanship of Viscount Ullswater was set up in 1921 'to inquire and report what, if any, alterations are needed in the local government of the administrative county of London and the surrounding district, with a view to securing greater efficiency and economy in the administration of local government services and to reducing any inequalities which may exist in the distribution of local burdens as between different parts of the whole area'. The Commission issued a Majority Report and two Minority Reports.

The members who signed the Majority Report recommended the retention of the existing structure. Although it was recognised that the area of the LCC no longer covered the whole of London's built-up area, and evidence was submitted in support of the contention that the County Council found itself at a disadvantage in administering some of its services within its restricted boundaries, the majority of the members of the Commission were not convinced that any alteration in the existing system would result in greater efficiency or economy. They contented themselves, therefore, with making recommendations of a comparatively minor character.

In the First Minority Report (the Hiley–Talbot Report) it was recommended that London should be defined as an area with boundaries approximately ten miles from Charing Cross; that this area should be divided into a number of county boroughs; and that the administration of some services—e.g. water supply, main drainage and tramways— should be left to a central authority for the whole of London. The Second Minority Report (the Donald–Walsh Report) contained recommendations involving changes of an even more drastic nature. It was considered that to meet the needs of London government a Greater London Council should be elected for the whole of the Metropolitan Police District; that this Greater London Council should be responsible for town planning, transport, hospitals, main drainage and water supply; and that the other main services should be administered jointly by the Greater London Council and the district authorities within its area.

Faced with three sets of recommendations from the Ullswater Commission and with conflicting proposals from the local authorities in the Greater London area, the Government of the day made practically no attempt to find a solution to London's problems, and more than a generation passed before the matter again received serious consideration. It was recognised that the LCC was administering an area which could only be described as inner London, and that its obsolete and artificial boundaries militated against administrative efficiency. The fear was expressed, however, that a Greater London Council, with its huge population and its immense financial resources, might, even if it had restricted powers, become a serious rival to Parliament. In recognition of its special problems, London was in 1945 excluded from the purview of the Local Government Boundary Commission, and Greater London was outside the jurisdiction of the English Local Government Commission which was set up under the provisions of the Local Government Act, 1958.

The Royal Commission on London Government

A Royal Commission to examine the system and working of local government in the Greater London area under the chairmanship of Sir Edwin Herbert, a former President of the Law Society, which was set up in 1957, issued its report in 1960. The terms of reference of the Commission excluded the administration of the police and of water.

The main features of the proposed new pattern of London government were the creation of a directly elected Greater London Council, which was to be responsible for those services which could be effectively performed over a large area, and the establishment of fifty-two second-tier authorities, which were to be called Greater London Boroughs. These second-tier authorities were to have a population of 100 000 to 250 000. The recommendations of the Royal Commission, however, were not accepted in their entirety. The proposals for the reform of London Government, which were set out in a Government White Paper issued in 1961, and which in substance are now contained in the London Government Act, 1963, differed materially from the Royal Commission's proposals, particularly in regard to the number and size of the London boroughs and the administration of education.

The effect of the Local Government Act, 1972, on London government

Although the Local Government Act, 1972, made no alteration to the structure of local government in London, which was settled by the London Government Act, 1963, many of the provisions of the Act of 1972 concerning the constitution and general powers of local authorities were applied to London. A number of changes, for example, relating to qualification and disqualification for membership, discharge of functions and appointment of committees and officers, financial matters and audit of accounts now apply to London as well as to the rest of the country. In addition, the powers and duties of local authorities in London were changed as a result of the passing of the National Health Service Reorganisation Act, 1973, and the Water Act, 1973. As a result of this legislation, the GLC is no longer responsible for the ambulance service, the school health service (ILEA), main drainage and sewage, and the London boroughs and the City Corporation no longer administer the personal health services.

The constitution of the Greater London Council

The most important provisions of the London Government Act, 1963, related to the abolition of the LCC, the Middlesex County Council and the metropolitan borough councils, and the establishment in their place of the Greater London Council, the Inner London Education Authority and the thirty-two London boroughs.

The GLC consists of ninety-two councillors, who are elected in May for a period of four years for single member electoral areas, which are parliamentary constituencies. All the councillors retire together. At present the council also includes fifteen aldermen, who will retain their seats until the next election of councillors in 1977, when the office of alderman of the GLC will cease to exist. Aldermen were elected by the councillors from the councillors or chosen from other persons of special experience. The Chairman of the GLC, as head of the largest municipality in the country, occupies a position of dignity and importance, and is entitled to be called 'the Right Honourable'. As he takes no part in political controversy, his position is not unlike that of Speaker of the House of Commons. There is also a Vice-Chairman, who is chosen by the majority party, and a Deputy Chairman, who is selected by the opposition. The Council meets every three weeks on Tuesday afternoon, except in recess periods. Both the majority and minority parties appoint members as whips, who are responsible for ensuring the smooth running of the party machines and the attendance of members at council and committee meetings. The management structure of the Council provides for fifteen committees, including a Policy and Resources Committee, which assesses overall objectives and exercises a decisive control of the allocation of resources to each service, including finance and staff. The Council's chief executive officer is the Director General and Clerk to the Council, and it is he who advises on general policy and acts as leader of the team of heads of departments, as Clerk to the Inner London Education Authority and as clerk to all the Council's committees.

The functions of the Greater London Council

Although a comprehensive list of the multifarious services administered by the GLC would be out of place in this book, a broad indication can be given of its powers and duties. The distribution of functions between the GLC and the London boroughs is somewhat similar to that between metropolitan county councils and metropolitan district councils outside London. The GLC is not in any sense 'big brother' to the London boroughs, and is not empowered to supervise their activities.

The GLC, as strategic planning authority, prepared the Greater London Development Plan, and the London boroughs must prepare local plans within the framework of the strategic plan. In addition to being the overall road traffic authority for Greater London, the GLC is responsible for the maintenance of the Thames bridges (except the four City bridges) and for the construction and maintenance of the metropolitan roads—i.e. the main thoroughfares except trunk roads—although the actual work of maintenance is carried out on an agency basis by the London boroughs. The GLC appoints the members of the London Transport Executive, which is responsible for the day-to-day management of the Executive's underground and central bus services, exercises control of the Executive in matters of general policy and is empowered to give public transport in the area financial help. This power enabled the GLC in 1973–4 to include the sum of £25 000 000 in its rating precepts for the purpose of maintaining public transport fares in London at their existing levels.

As the largest municipal landlord in the world, the Council now still owns and manages about 200 000 homes, despite the fact that in recent years responsibility for a large number of houses and flats has been transferred to the London boroughs. One of the largest and most ambitious housing projects ever undertaken by a local authority is Thamesmead, which is on the site of the Royal Arsenal at Woolwich and Erith Marshes. This development, which is in course of construction, is expected to provide about 13 600 homes for 48 500 residents. The GLC also provides homes for Londoners in expanding towns and new towns, some of which are far removed from London, and in this way the pressure on housing in London is considerably relieved.

Other functions of the GLC include the maintenance of the regional parks (some parks formerly maintained by the GLC having been transferred to the London boroughs), the administration of the fire service, refuse disposal, the licensing of places of public entertainment, betting tracks and petroleum installations, and (as agents for the Department of the Environment) motor vehicles and drivers. In

Inner London the Council also controls the construction of buildings. The Council maintains a research and intelligence organisation with power to collect the information required for the planning of London's services.

The Inner London Education Authority

The Inner London Education Authority is a special committee of the GLC with virtually autonomous powers, and the two bodies work in close co-operation with each other. The ILEA is responsible for education in the City and in the twelve inner London boroughs—i.e. approximately the area formerly administered by the LCC. The Authority consists of the thirty-five members of the GLC representing the inner area, one representative appointed by each of the inner London boroughs and one by the City of London Corporation. The ILEA, however, has an education committee, consisting of these forty-eight members and of seventeen other persons experienced in education, five of whom are teachers employed by the Authority.

The finances of the Greater London Council

When the Council wishes to borrow money for its capital expenditure, unlike other local authorities it obtains consent to the loan not from the Secretary of State for the Environment but by promoting an annual Money Bill in Parliament. The GLC is empowered to promote Bills in Parliament for any purpose which is for the public benefit of the inhabitants, and in the Council's annual General Powers Act there are provisions relating to the London boroughs and the City of London Corporation.

An indication of the wide scope of the functions of the GLC, and the extent to which they impinge on the daily life of the Londoner, may be gathered from the relevant financial statistics. The estimated penny rate product for Greater London in 1974–5 is £18 350 000. The GLC (including the ILEA) budget for 1974–5 amounts to about £984 million, of which £742 million was revenue expenditure and £242 million capital expenditure. In 1975–6 expenditure is likely to be much higher. There are many sovereign states which are members of the United Nations but are in no position to incur expenditure on this vast scale.

The London borough councils

Under the London Government Act, 1963, Greater London comprises the City of London and thirty-two London boroughs (twelve in inner London and twenty in outer London). Most of these boroughs have sixty councillors and ten aldermen. Under the Local Government Act, 1972, the councillors are elected in May for a period of four years, and all the councillors retire together. The next election will be held in 1978, and the aldermen will retain their seats until that date, after which the office of alderman in London boroughs will cease to exist.

The London boroughs and the City Corporation share responsibility with the GLC for solving the acute housing problems of Greater London. They provide new homes within their areas, undertake improvement schemes and slum clearance, and advance money to people who wish to buy their own homes. Their powers and duties include the administration of the services relating to the welfare of aged and disabled persons and deprived children. The functions of the London boroughs also include environmental health, libraries, entertainments, and the construction, maintenance and lighting of highways, for which they have direct responsibility or act as agents for the GLC or the Department of the Environment. In addition, they have powers in relation to parks and open spaces, and deal with applications for planning permission and the preparation of local plans. Other borough functions are the administration of the legislation relating to shops and offices, food and drugs, weights and measures, consumer services, the registration of electors, and the registration of births, deaths and marriages. The outer London boroughs are local education authorities, but in inner London the education service is administered by the ILEA. Although the outer London boroughs control the construction of buildings and enforce building standards, this function (subject to certain powers of delegation to the boroughs) is in inner London the responsibility of the GLC.

There is a London Boroughs Association, a voluntary body established in 1964, on which each of the London boroughs and the City Corporation are represented. Each of the London boroughs also belongs to a national organisation—the Association of Metropolitan Authorities—as well as to the LBA.

The City of London Corporation

The City has no Charter of Incorporation, but it has been granted numerous charters by various monarchs, starting with William the Conqueror. Throughout its history the wealth and prestige of the City have enabled it to resist with success any proposal to encroach on its traditional rights and privileges. The City was excluded from the provisions of the Municipal Corporations Act, 1835, and when the Metropolitan Board of Works was established in 1855 the control of the Board over the City was limited to the running of the main drains through the square mile. From 1866 the Board was entrusted with the duty of extinguishing fires throughout its area, including the City. Owing to determined opposition from the City Corporation in 1884, a Bill to reform London government failed to reach the statute book, and the Report of a Royal Commission in 1895, which recommended the abolition of the City and its incorporation in the County of London, encountered resistance from the Corporation, with the result that the proposal came to nothing.

The constitution of the City of London is unique among English municipalities. There are three courts or assemblies, each of which plays its part in the government of the City. The Court of Common Hall consists of the Lord Mayor, sheriffs, aldermen and liverymen—i.e. those members of the City companies who have the right to wear the livery of their company and are freemen of the City. The Court of Common Hall elects the sheriffs and every year submits the names of two aldermen who have held the office of sheriff to the Court of Aldermen, which then makes a selection of one of these aldermen as Lord Mayor. The Court of Aldermen, which is the only surviving example of a municipal second chamber, consists of the Lord Mayor and the twenty-five other aldermen, who are elected for life by the local government electors. Each alderman is *ex-officio* a justice of the peace for the City, and the Lord Mayor is chief magistrate. There has never been a woman alderman of the City. In 1973 the only woman to be elected by the ward voters was refused admission to the Court of Aldermen. The main governing body of the City is, however, the Court of Common Council. This body consists of the Lord Mayor, aldermen and 159 common councillors. These common councillors are elected by persons who are resident in or occupy premises in the City of the yearly value of at least £10.

The offices held by the principal officers of the Corporation are mainly of great antiquity. The Recorder, for example, who is appointed for life by the Court of Aldermen, besides being the senior law officer, is a judge of the Central Criminal Court (held at the Old Bailey), which is the Crown Court sitting in the City. The responsibilities of the Town Clerk are similar to those of other town clerks and chief executive officers. The Remembrancer is the parliamentary officer.

Until the coming into operation of the London Government Act, 1963, which reformed London government, the functions of the City of London Corporation, although wider than those of a metropolitan borough council, were far less extensive than those of a county borough council, as many important powers and duties in the City were exercised by the LCC. In addition to the functions discharged by the metropolitan borough councils, the City Corporation controlled its own police force, maintained the City bridges, and administered the Shops Acts and the Acts dealing with weights and measures and the storage of petroleum. The Corporation also maintained Epping Forest, Burnham Beeches and West Ham Park, and had control over markets, including Smithfields, Billingsgate and Spitalfields, within seven miles of its boundaries.

Under the 1963 legislation, which reorganised London government, the Corporation retained nearly all its existing powers and duties and acquired new functions, including the personal health and welfare services and the care of deprived children. All the local government services in the City are administered either by the City Corporation or by the GLC, and education is the responsibility of the ILEA. Since the coming into operation of the National Health Service Reorganisation Act, 1973, the Corporation has not been responsible for the administration of the personal health services. No changes were made in the City boundaries.

The equalisation of rates

The rating authorities in Greater London are the City Corporation and the London borough councils. The London boroughs levy rates to meet their own requirements and those of the Thames Water Authority, and the precepts of the GLC and of the Metropolitan Police; and the City Corporation is in a similar position, except that as it manages its own police force it is not required to meet precepts from the Metropolitan Police.

The rates in the £ payable in the City of London and in the London boroughs are to some extent equalised by the operation of a pooling scheme under which the more affluent boroughs and the City Corporation render assistance to boroughs in need of financial help. As a result of this scheme, there is a greater measure of uniformity of rate poundages in Greater London than there is in the rest of the country.

Under a new equalisation scheme approved in 1974, all the inner and outer London boroughs contribute a rate of 2p in the £, and this total is distributed to outer London boroughs on a population basis. Under the revised scheme, the City of London Corporation and the City of Westminster have fared considerably worse.

Other authorities concerned with London government

Reference has already been made to the Metropolitan Police and to the London Transport Executive. Other authorities which are or have been concerned with London government include the Metropolitan Water Board, the Port of London Authority and the Conservators of the River Thames.

The Metropolitan Water Board, which was set up under the Metropolis Water Act, 1902, consisted of thirty-nine members, appointed by the constituent authorities in the London area. The members of the Board held office for three years. The Board was established because of complaints that the water supplied by the private companies which had previously undertaken this function was impure and inadequate. The heavy compensation paid to the water companies created considerable financial difficulties for the Board during the first years of its existence, but before long the Board was able to provide an adequate supply of pure water to the domestic consumer at a reasonable cost. Under the Water Act, 1973, the functions of the Board and of the Conservators of the River Thames, which controlled the River from Teddington to the source, were transferred to the Thames Water Authority, some of whose members are appointed by the London borough councils and the City Corporation.

The Port of London Authority was created by the Port of London Act, 1908. The functions of the Authority had previously been discharged by private companies who owned the docks. The PLA is concerned with the control of the Port, including the docks, and of the Thames from Teddington to the sea. For sanitary purposes, however, the City Corporation is the port health authority. The members of the Authority are appointed by the Department of the Environment after consultation with the various bodies concerned with the port industry, including the GLC and the City of London Corporation.

Books for Further Reading

Cross, C. A., *Principles of Local Government Law*. Sweet & Maxwell (1974).

Cross, C. A., *The Local Government Act, 1972*. Sweet & Maxwell (1973).

Freeman, R., *Becoming a Councillor*. Charles Knight (1970).

Glendinning, J. and Bullock, R., *Management by Objectives in Local Government*. Charles Knight (1974).

Golding, L., *A Dictionary of Local Government in England and Wales*. English Universities Press (1962).

Hall, Penelope, *Social Services of England and Wales*, edited by Anthony Forder. Routledge & Kegan Paul (1969).

Hart, W., and Garner, J., *Introduction to the Law of Local Government and Administration*. Butterworth (1973).

Jackson, R., *The Machinery of Local Government*. Macmillan (1968).

Jackson, W., *Achievement:* A short History of the London County Council. Longmans (1965).

Jewell, R., *Central and Local Government*. Charles Knight (1970).

Keith-Lucas, B., *The English Local Government Franchise*. Basil Blackwell (1952).

Knowles, R., *Modern Management in Local Government*. Butterworth (1971).

Laski, H., *A Century of Municipal Progress*. Allen & Unwin (1936).

Mackintosh, J., *The Devolution of Power*. Chatto & Windus (1968).

Rhodes, G., and Ruck, S., *The Government of Greater London*. Allen & Unwin (1970).

Richards, P., *The Reformed Local Government System*. Allen & Unwin (1974).

Robson, W., *Local Government in Crisis*. Allen & Unwin (1969).

Robson, W., *The Government and Misgovernment of London*. Allen & Unwin (1948).

Rose, B., *The Councillor's Work*. Charles Knight (1971).

Schofield, N., *The Councillor*. Shaw (1970).

Smellie, K., *A History of Local Government*. Allen & Unwin (1968).

Stewart, J., *Management in Local Government*, Charles Knight (1971).

Tate, W., *The Parish Chest*. Cambridge University Press (1969).

Webb, S. and B., *The Development of Local Government*, 9 volumes. Frank Cass (reprinted 1963).

Willmott, Phyllis, *The Consumers' Guide to the British Social Services*. Penguin (1973).

Central Office of Information, *Local Government in Britain*. HMSO (1972).

Scheme of Conditions of Service. National Joint Council for Local Authorities' Administrative, Professional, Technical and Clerical Services (1971).

Greater London Services 1974–75. Greater London Council.

Index

TEACH YOURSELF BOOKS

THE LAW

J. Leigh Mellor

This book is an introductory guide to the fundamental principles of English law. In intelligible
language it explains the basis and development of
English law up to and including in this new edition
the present day. Aspects of law covered include: the
history of English law – constitutional law – property law – matrimonial causes – wills and trusts –
criminal law – evidence and civil procedure – juries
judges, the legal profession, legal aid.

As a guide to English law for the ordinary man
or woman, this book will prove invaluable, but it is
also an important and valuable introductory survey
of law for the student.

75p

ISBN 0 340 18262 8

TEACH YOURSELF BOOKS

BRITISH CONSTITUTION

R. E. C. Jewell

This book provides a comprehensive account of the
evolution of the British Constitution and an overall
picture of the present constitutional position. The
author has broken this down for the student into
detailed but manageable components, covered in
separate chapters ranging from the Royal Prerog-
ative and the Sovereignty of Parliament to the
Judiciary and the Commonwealth. This new edition incorporates all statutory and constitutional
changes up to and including March 1975.

An inclusive account of the nature and workings
of the British Constitution, written as a text for
students of the subject at GCE 'A' Level and as a
valuable introduction for students of law and
history.

£1·25

ISBN 0 340 19820 6

LEISURE, DOMESTIC & GENERAL
TITLES IN TEACH YOURSELF BOOKS

Care and Welfare

All these books are avilable at your bookshop or newsagent or can be ordered direct from the publisher: Teach Yourself Books, P.O. Box 11, Falmouth, Cornwall.

Please send cheque or postal order. No currency, and allow the following for postage and packing:

1 book – 10p, 2 books – 15p, 3 books – 20p, 4–5 books – 25p, 6–9 books – 4p per copy, 10–15 books – 2½p per copy, 16–30 books – 2p per copy, over 30 books free within the U.K.

Overseas – please allow 10p for the first book and 5p per copy for each additional book.

While every effort is made to keep prices low, it is sometimes necessary to increase prices at short notice. Teach Yourself Books reserve the right to show new retail prices on covers which may differ from those previously advertised in the text or elsewhere.